Peter
the
Rock

EXTRAORDINARY INSIGHTS FROM AN ORDINARY MAN

David W. Gill

INTERVARSITY PRESS
DOWNERS GROVE, ILLINOIS 60515

InterVarsity Press is the book-publishing division of Inter-Varsity Christian Fellowship, a student movement active on campus at hundreds of universities, colleges and schools of nursing. For information about local and regional activities, write IVCF, 233 Langdon St., Madison, WI 53703.

Distributed in Canada through InterVarsity Press, 860 Denison St., Unit 3, Markham, Ontario L3R 4H1, Canada.

All Scripture quotations, unless otherwise indicated, are from the Holy Bible, New International Version. Copyright © 1973, 1978, International Bible Society. Used by permission of Zondervan Bible Publishers.

Cover illustration: Roberta Polfus

ISBN 0-87784-609-X

Printed in the United States of America

Library of Congress Cataloging in Publication Data
Gill, David W., 1946-

  Peter the rock.

  Bibliography: p.
  1. Peter, the Apostle, Saint.   I. Title.
BS2515.G53   1986   255.9'24   86-7383
ISBN 0-87784-609-X

17	16	15	14	13	12	11	10	9	8	7	6	5	4	3	2	1
99	98	97	96	95	94	93	92	91	90	89	88	87	86			

For
my parents
Walter and Vivian Gill
and
my children
Jodie and Jonathan Gill

Preface

I have two interconnected purposes for writing this book. First, I want to explore anew the meaning of Christianity. What does it mean to become a Christian? What does it mean to live as a Christian in the church and the world? I am well aware, of course, of the countless discussions of these questions over the centuries and I have neither illusions nor intentions that mine will represent any significant new departures. In fact, my goal is simply to restate, as faithfully as possible, the essential features of biblical Christianity.

There is much to be gained by studying the Christian writings of the past, especially the great classics of the faith. Nevertheless, it falls to each generation to rearticulate the truth of the gospel. The substance remains the same because God's revelation has been fully and decisively given in Jesus Christ and Scripture. But the forms in which this substance is expressed must change somewhat for two reasons. First, our ears become dulled through the repeated hearing of old formulations. Second, languages and cultural contexts vary over time and space; what communicates well in one situation or generation may fail to do so in another. It is the glory of Christianity that God himself enters into our history. This was true above all in the incarnation of God in Jesus Christ. But it is also true that God can and will speak to us in our own time, place and language.

My parents taught me the Word of God when I was a child. It falls to me to teach my own children, to be a bridge between these two generations, across which the gospel might travel. In part, this book is a grateful "confession of faith" dedicated to my parents. With still more passion, it is dedicated to my two teen-agers, Jodie and Jonathan, to whom I am currently attempting to pass on "the way, the truth, and the life" in Jesus Christ. As I have written this book, I have also thought of aggressive questions posed by inner-city youths in Bible studies I led for five years at the Alameda County Juvenile Hall, of discussions and debates with various religious and secular individuals in Berkeley over the past twenty years, and of questioning, anxiety-ridden fellow Christians who have spent hours in my office or home trying to work through the meaning of their (sometimes imperiled) faith. So it is not just for my children or my parents but for all such questioners and searchers, Christian or not, that I have undertaken this study. My hope is that it can serve as a kind of introductory handbook on Christian discipleship, both for individual study and group discussion. The three questions "for reflection and discussion" at the close of each chapter are intended to stimulate your thinking beyond what I have written. Many of the books cited in the footnotes are mentioned more to suggest resources for your further study than to buttress my own arguments.

As indicated earlier (and from the title of the book), there is a second purpose for writing this book, interwoven with the first. I wish to explore the meaning of Christianity by studying the life and letters of Simon Peter. I want to trail him through the New Testament. Since my late teens and early twenties I have sensed a special affinity for this New Testament character, and I have come to regard him as a close brother and a beloved teacher—my "mentor" in the Christian faith, if you will. This book is my effort to share with you what I have learned from him.

In the first chapter I will explain more fully the promise of this focus on Peter as well as the method by which I will carry it out. By no means do I propose that either the focus on Peter or the method of my study are the only way to get at the essential character of Christianity. Numerous valuable studies, for example, have centered on Jesus or Paul or on one passage or book. Without minimizing these contributions, I want to propose Peter's life and teaching as another, extremely illuminating avenue to the truth of Christianity. My contribution to biblical studies will be modest at best. I am a Christian ethicist and not a highly trained biblical technician or New Testament historian. Still, I am convinced of the value of the kind of "lay" discussion which follows.

While I am responsible for any weaknesses or mistakes which you find in this study, I must share credit with several others for whatever you find of lasting value. My parents, Walter and Vivian Gill, were my first and best teachers. By their lives as well as their words, they taught me the power of the gospel and the desirability of a life with Jesus Christ. I also owe more than I can say to a humble, little-known servant of God named Clarence Mayo, who pastored me through good times and bad in high school and university. He knew the Bible from cover to cover and, more importantly, walked more constantly and closely with Jesus Christ than anyone I have ever known.

I have valued the encouragement and criticism of my ideas on Peter from my home congregation, Berkeley Covenant Church, and also from Inter-Varsity Christian Fellowship groups on many university campuses. An adult study group (taught with Bill Moore) at Oakland First Covenant Church and another at the San Francisco Careers Fellowship each gave three months' attention and response to this material in an earlier form. Jennifer Adams, Michael Maudlin, Jim Sire and my wife Lucia each contributed helpful suggestions and encouragement after reading the penultimate manuscript. North Park Theological Seminary Professor of New Testament Klyne Snodgrass contributed a careful critique and saved me from several errors—though I am sure he will remain uneasy with some of what I argue.

I am grateful to New College Berkeley for allowing me a sabbatical leave in 1984-85, without which this study could not have been completed. My debts to many other scholars and writers will be apparent in the footnotes and text. Chief among these is Jacques Ellul, with whom I met regularly during a year in Bordeaux. His insight and encouragement were a great help to this study of Peter—as they have been in virtually all of my work over the past fifteen years. As a prophetic voice speaking the Word of God to our era, he has few peers.

David W. Gill
Bordeaux, France
Pentecost 1985

1 The Promise of Peter: An Introduction

*"On this rock I will build
my church, and the gates of Hades
will not overcome it."*

HE WAS JUST AN ORDINARY GUY, A WORKING MAN, A FISHERMAN TO BE precise.[1] No distinguished family name—all we know for sure is that his father was called John! Not a lot of money and not much in the way of formal education, it seems. Like all "ordinary people" he had his particular strengths and he had his share of human weakness. His life revolved around the family business, the sea, the wife, the mother-in-law—you know the kind of story.

And yet, as a result of meeting and then following Jesus of Nazareth for three years or so, this ordinary guy became one of the key figures in the history of the world. Writers, painters, sculptors and countless others have been inspired or captivated by what they know about him. It would be very hard to find anyone who knew the bare minimum about Christianity who would not know his name and one or two stories about him. Unquestionably, some profound and far-reaching changes occurred in this man's life as a result of Jesus. But we never lose sight of the fact that Peter remains an ordinary person—like us—

in whom these extraordinary changes take place.

When we first encounter Peter in the New Testament, he is a fisher-man living and working in Galilee, the region of Palestine north of Samaria and Judea. The year is approximately A.D. 27. His given name was Simon.

Jesus of Nazareth gave him the name *Peter* (Mt 16:18; Mk 3:16; Jn 1:42). While we are accustomed to hearing this as a common name, when Simon received it the word simply meant "the Rock." The early disciples knew this man as "Simon the Rock," or more simply as "Rocky" or "the Rock"! Simon was sometimes called "Cephas," from the Aramaic word *kepha*, meaning "rock" or "stone." Because his father's name was John, his full name would be Simon "the Rock" Johnson. This name helps us grasp how people in the first century would react on being introduced to him. It is only out of respect for tradition, and a wish not to appear flippant, that I will continue to call him Peter instead of the more accurate Simon "the Rock" Johnson!

Peter was from Bethsaida ("fisherman's city") and Capernaum, neighboring towns on the eastern bank of the Jordan River where it empties into the Sea of Galilee. Bethsaida was a Jewish city with Greek influence. One scholar has argued: "Anyone brought up in Bethsaida would not only have understood Greek but would also have been polished by intercourse with foreigners and have had some Greek culture."[2] Whatever we make of that claim, it is clear that though Peter was intelligent, he "had not 'studied' either by Jewish or Greek standards."[3] Peter and John were characterized as "unschooled" by the religious leadership in Jerusalem (Acts 4:13) because they were not technically trained in the rabbinic schools—though their Galilean accent may have been an additional source of this contempt they faced.

Throughout his adult life we may guess that Peter was married. The healing of his mother-in-law comes at the beginning of his relation-ship with Jesus. Twenty years later Paul mentioned that Peter custom-arily took his wife with him on his missionary travels (see Mk 1:30; Lk 4:38; 1 Cor 9:5).

The two sons of John, Peter and Andrew, worked with the two sons of Zebedee, John and James, in a fishing partnership (Lk 5:10). All four got their hands dirty in the daily work. When they began following Jesus, Zebedee and "the hired servants" took care of the business (Mk 1:20). I am inclined to think that Peter remained active as a fisherman even after his primary attention shifted to the work of Jesus of Nazareth (see Mt 17:27; Jn 21:3), just as Paul, for example, worked as a "tentmaker" while an apostle (Acts 18:3; 1 Cor 9:6).

In Peter's day, Palestine was a province under the thumb of the Roman Empire. Although the Jews were allowed to retain their own king (from the family of Herod during this era), a Roman governor, Pontius Pilate, and resident Roman troops were a frequent irritation to the local population. Jewish "parties" like the Pharisees, Sadducees, Zealots and Essenes, represented not only different religious viewpoints but also different views on how to relate to the occupying Roman colonizers.[4]

We don't know whether Peter was very political or religious. In any event it was his brother Andrew and their fishing partner, John, who investigated the wild prophet out of the desert, John the Baptist, and became disciples of this forerunner of Jesus. It was through Andrew that Peter met Jesus and eventually became his follower, along with James and John. This foursome must have constituted a rather interesting business partnership! James and John were given the nickname *Sons of Thunder* by Jesus, perhaps because of their exuberant, aggressive spirit (Mt 3:17). At one point Jesus had to rebuke their misguided zeal, when they wished to call down fire from heaven to consume some unrepentant Samaritans (Lk 9:54-55)! Just as Peter was transformed from a "stumbling block" into a solid foundation rock for the church, so also John was transformed from a person of passionate, thunderous violence into the great teacher of passionate, thunderous love.[5] Andrew's career and life are unreported after the first chapter of Acts. James met with martyrdom sometime between A.D. 41-44 under Herod Agrippa I (Acts 12:2).

After beginning their three-year association with Jesus of Nazareth, Peter, James and John became the inner circle of Jesus' followers. These three alone accompanied Jesus into the house of Jairus, the synagogue leader whose daughter Jesus raised from the dead (Mk 5:37; Lk 8:51). They alone were with Jesus on the mountain when he was "transfigured" (Mt 17:1; Mk 9:2; Lk 9:28). And they alone were with Jesus in his distress in the garden of Gethsemane (Mt 26:37; Mk 14:33). Why were they so special? In my judgment it was simply because they *wanted* to be near Jesus more consistently and enthusiastically than did the others. Reckless enthusiasm to be near Jesus paid off then (as it does now).

Within this inner circle, it was Peter who dominated the story, according to all four Gospels. He often articulated the questions or attempted a response to Jesus' questions. He alone attempted to walk on the water (Mt 14:28). It was Peter who made the great confession of faith at Caesarea Philippi leading to Jesus' famous "on this rock I will build my church" (Mt 16:18). Both on this occasion and a week later on the Mount of Transfiguration Peter also made his presence felt negatively and received some of the severest rebukes possible (Mt 16:23; 17:5). In the upper room where the disciples met with Jesus on the night he was betrayed, it was Peter who balked at having his feet washed by Jesus and who boasted that he would never deny Jesus (Jn 13; Mk 14:29-31). Later that night Peter alone lifted the sword in an attempt (misguided, to be sure) to prevent Jesus' arrest (Jn 18:10). When most of the other disciples ran away, Peter followed Jesus to his trial—only to deny him in the clutch (Lk 22:54-62). Little wonder then that the disciples were sometimes called "Peter and his companions" (Mt 17:24; Mk 1:36; Lk 9:32). In all of this, however, Peter's role was not that of leader in the sense of "director" or "boss." Rather, Peter was the spokesman, the representative and the modeler of the life of the disciples. He was a paradigm of the life of a follower of Jesus, both in his strength and weakness.

After the death of Jesus, Peter was the first to enter the empty tomb and the first apostolic witness of the resurrected Christ (Lk 24:34; Jn 20:6; 1 Cor 15:5). Recovered from his great denial of Christ, Peter became the most prominent leader of the early church in Jerusalem and preached the first great public messages about Jesus Christ, beginning on the day of Pentecost (Acts 1—2). Accompanied by his old friend John, Peter carried forward the preaching and healing ministry of Jesus in remarkable fashion (Acts 3). When Saul of Tarsus was converted a few years later, he came to see Peter for fifteen days of orientation to the Christian way of Jesus (Gal 1:18). With James, the Lord's brother, assuming an increasing burden of the pastoral leadership of the Jerusalem church, Peter enlarged his missionary travels and eventually became known as the apostle to the Jews (Gal 2:7). Though Paul, in turn, became the leading apostle to the Gentiles, this role definition was not precise in a growing church that broke down such racial and cultural barriers. Thus one of the first prominent gentile conversions in the Acts story was brought about by Peter's visit to the Roman centurion Cornelius (Acts 10).

Just after the execution of his friend James, Peter himself was jailed to await execution by Herod Agrippa I in the early 40s. After a miraculous escape from prison, Peter went briefly to meet with the Christians at the home of Mary, Mark's mother, then "left for another place" (Acts 12:17). Apart from his active participation in the "Council of Jerusalem" (late 40s probably; Acts 15), we cannot trace his steps with certainty for the remainder of his life. It seems very likely that Peter spent time in northern Asia Minor because his first letter was addressed to Christians in "Pontus, Galatia, Cappadocia, Asia and Bithynia" (1 Pet 1:1). That he visited Corinth (at least) in Greece seems implied by Paul's first letter to the Corinthians in which he rebuked a sectarian "I am of Cephas" spirit and also mentioned Peter's habit of taking his wife along on his travels, as though they knew of this practice (1 Cor 1:12; 9:5). My guess is that from about A.D. 44-62 Peter was primarily engaged in Christian mission and church planting (and nurturing) outside of Jerusalem, perhaps with a special interest in the movement in northern Asia Minor.

Finally, it is all but certain that Peter wrote his first letter (to the churches of northern Asia Minor) from Rome (the meaning of "Babylon" in 1 Pet 5:13), editorially assisted by Silas (*Silvanus*, (1 Pet 5:12), the sometime editorial assistant and companion of Paul. It is also noteworthy that Peter signs off this letter with greetings from "my son Mark" (1 Pet 5:13). According to Papias, a bishop in Phrygia writing in A.D. 132, Mark was the "interpreter of Peter" who "wrote down accurately everything he remembered without however recording in order what was either said or done by Christ." During the century after Papias, Irenaeus of Lyons and Tertullian of Carthage also said

Mark's Gospel was based on Peter's word. Eusebius, the great church historian of the fourth century, and Jerome at the beginning of the fifth century added their voices in support of this view of Mark.

You may recall that Paul and Barnabas had a sharp parting of the ways over Paul's insistence that Mark not accompany them on a voyage because he had unexpectedly "deserted them" in the middle of a previous trip (Acts 15:38). A little impetuous? Think also of the literary style of Mark's Gospel—crisp, fast-moving, bristling with action and with words like *immediately*. It doesn't take a genius to see in this Gospel echoes, perhaps, of Peter's own eagerness and impulsiveness. Maybe old Peter was temperamentally better suited to have the younger, perhaps volatile, Mark under his wing than was Paul.

It is all but impossible that Peter could have founded the church at Rome or (still less likely) served as its "bishop" at some point. However, it is quite thinkable that Peter and others (including Paul, Mark, Silas and Luke) were all drawn to Rome in the early sixties. These were stormy times for the church: Paul's arrest and appeal to Caesar brought him to Rome under house arrest. James, the Lord's brother and a pillar of the church in Jerusalem, was executed in A.D. 62. Persecution of Christians, which had been sporadic, was going to become intense under the Emperor Nero beginning in the summer of A.D. 64. It was, I suspect, in these circumstances in Rome that Peter gave Mark material for his Gospel and also wrote his first letter to his beleaguered friends in northern Asia Minor urging them to faithfulness in spite of suffering (with editorial assistance from Silas, which may explain the marvelous Greek and the stylistic affinities with Paul's letters).[6]

The historical evidence grows dimmer still at this point. My guess is that within a year after completing his first letter, word reached Peter in Rome that things were worse than expected in the churches of northern Asia Minor. Perhaps to evade suffering, some in these churches were falling prey to false teaching which reduced Christianity into a combination of mystical "wisdom" and conformist, worldly living. Hearing this, Peter prepared a second letter which was only edited and circulated after his death by a new "editorial assistant" (which explains its radically different Greek style).[7]

With regard to Peter's death, the great New Testament scholar Oscar Cullmann concluded: the evidence is "sufficient to let us include the martyrdom of Peter in Rome in our final historical picture of the early Church as a fact which is relatively though not absolutely assured." What evidence there is suggests that in Nero's persecution Peter was betrayed by certain jealous brothers in the church and died by crucifixion in A.D. 64 or 65. It is possible that Peter could see it coming even while writing his first letter: "I appeal as . . . a witness of Christ's sufferings and one who also will share in the glory to be revealed" (1 Pet 5:1). The word "witness" (Greek, *martys*) was still closely identified with the idea of going to a martyr's death. So too John, writing much later, recalled the words of the Lord to Peter: "When you are old you will stretch out your hands, and someone else will dress you and lead you where you do not want to go" (Jn 21:18).[8]

There are many gaps and uncertainties confronting anyone who wishes to write a biography of Simon Peter. This is especially true for the period before he met Jesus in the late twenties and for the time after he left Jerusalem in the forties and disappeared from the story in Luke's Acts of the Apostles. Still, his presence looms across the pages of the New Testament for a period of fifteen or twenty years in a way which has made a decisive contribution to Christianity and history in the more than nineteen hundred years since then. And he was just an ordinary guy who met Jesus!

Why Peter?

Christianity is about Jesus Christ. Whatever else it may be—a philosophy of life, a style of living, a theology of history—it is fundamentally a message: the good news of Jesus Christ. Christians are ordinary human beings who come to know God in Jesus Christ. The challenge of the Christian life is to *know* Jesus Christ as fully and clearly as possible and to *follow* him as faithfully as possible in daily life. Christians are people who acknowledge that "in the past God spoke . . . at many times and in various ways" but believe that he has spoken most clearly and decisively in Jesus Christ, "the exact representation of his being," the Savior of all who are lost, the Creator and Lord of all, the Teacher and Pattern of God's word and will (Heb 1:1-3). Our primary attention as Christians, then, is focused on Jesus Christ.

In a very important sense the Christian life can be described as obedience to the teaching of Jesus Christ and imitation of his example. Thus, it is essential that we have various careful studies of the life and teaching of Jesus. A major reason why we *can* follow Jesus in this world is that he really was "made like his brothers in every way" (Heb 2:17). In fact he was "tempted in every way, just as we are" (Heb 4:15). However, Jesus remains a unique case because, as the text just cited adds, he was in all of this "without sin." He is the perfect standard. We want to be, and must seek to be, closely attached to him. But Jesus remains the "followed" more than the "follower." We find that we fall short of any sort of easy conformity to our Lord. Our successes are inexorably mixed in with many failures.

Jesus Christ was, is and always will be the center of Christian faith and life. After Jesus' death, resurrection and ascension, however, it was Paul who eventually became the dominant visible figure in the first-century church. He became *the* missionary, *the* teacher and theologian, and *the* leader of the expanding, maturing Christian movement. For every book on Peter, James or John, there are ten on Paul. There is no minimizing Paul's importance. For Martin Luther, John Wesley, Karl Barth and countless others, Paul's writings (and example) have brought about the decisive revolution in their lives, opening mind and heart to Jesus Christ.

Nevertheless, Paul comes across to many Christians as being in a kind of special, saintly class with few other members. Where are the New Testament stories of Paul's failures and recoveries? He is, by all accounts, brilliant, righteous, self-disciplined, austere, celibate, courageous, indefatigable and holy. He is right most or all of the time. It doesn't help much to hear him confess that he is "the chief of sinners" or struggles with a "thorn in the flesh." Though these are, no doubt, heavy and regrettable burdens, he handles them too easily, righteously and successfully for many of us to closely identify with him.[9]

And then there is Simon Peter. From his first encounter with Jesus to his last word in the New Testament era, I see a man I can truly call my brother, bone of my bones and flesh of my flesh. This disciple knows where I have been! His love and passion for Jesus Christ are transparently obvious. His reckless faith in the power of God inspires me. At the same time his stumbling and bumbling, his weaknesses and denials, reflect the kind of struggles I have from day to day. The challenge of the Christian life will always be to know and walk with Jesus Christ. For us ordinary mortals, pursuing this challenge with Peter as our brother and teacher is a most helpful, encouraging and gratifying adventure.

It is extremely reassuring to us, as it must have been for the people of Israel, that God calls himself "the God of Jacob" so often in the Old Testament (for example, Ex 3:6). Jacob, the conniving, deceitful "supplanter" was given a new name of promise and hope, *Israel*. But God does not just identify himself as "the God of Israel"! He is always also the God of Jacob, the God who welcomes and redeems ordinary people with extraordinary faults. So too, Jesus is the Savior and Lord of Simon Peter, warts and all. God built his chosen people Israel out of Jacob, and he builds his church on a foundation of apostolic rocks like Peter.

The Promise of Peter
The promise of focusing a study of Christianity on Peter has at least three aspects. First, Peter illuminates a broad spectrum of human and Christian experience with which ordinary people can readily identify. By this I do not mean that people "ordinarily" walk on water or see Christ transfigured! But we encounter Peter as a novice follower of Jesus, and we may trail him through his years into maturity as a veteran leader. We may observe him in his daring risks of faith and read his seasoned observations on theological issues. We may see him in his failures—and in his recovery from failure. We see him when he is brave and when he is fearful. He "leaves all" to follow Jesus— but he's got a wife, a brother and friends along with him! (And thus we must be careful to understand what "leaving all" really means.) In short, the struggles and circumstances of our contemporary existence as Christians often find clear and helpful counterparts in the saga of Peter.

A second aspect to the promise of Peter has to do with the way his portrait cuts across the New Testament canon as no other. Not only scholars but ordinary Christians need ways to come to terms with the diversity of the twenty-seven books in the New Testament while discerning the unity that binds together this collection. The most obvious point in this regard is that Peter is the one figure who looms large during the earthly ministry of Jesus described in the Gospels *as well as* the post-Pentecost church in which Paul becomes the dominant figure. Peter is a promising "bridge" between Gospels and Letters, between Jesus and Paul. What changes? What remains the same?

So too, Peter cuts across all four Gospels as an avenue of comparative study. In each Gospel different Peter-incidents are reported—or the same ones are reported but with different details and purposes. Peter figures in the earliest letter (Galatians) and the earliest Gospel (Mark, probably as the major source for the author), and his name is attached to the last, most controversial document admitted into the canon, 2 Peter. Certainly the most vigorous recent statement of this promise from the scholarly world is the conclusion of James D. G. Dunn's *Unity and Diversity in the New Testament:* "Peter . . . became the focal point of unity in the great Church, since *Peter was probably in fact and effect the bridge-man who did more than any other to hold together the diversity of first-century Christianity.*"[10] Put in other terms, if you want to get a handle on the New Testament, Peter is a promising means.

While Peter is thus a promising link between the key personalities and the various books of the New Testament, he also holds promise by way of illuminating most of the key topics or issues in Christian ethics, theology and discipleship. He has not authored numerous or lengthy theological treatises like Paul. But consider an issue such as conversion. In the New Testament we not only have four reports of Peter's first encounter and decision to follow Jesus, we also have descriptions in Acts of his own efforts to win converts, and we have his mature observations on the topic in his first letter. Or consider politics: again we have Peter's own encounters with the political powers in the Gospels and Acts, and we have his teaching in 1 Peter. Developing a biblical view of politics and the state requires Peter's contribution—not just a quick resort to Paul's famous text in Romans 13. So too, the most frequently quoted text to justify the Christian apologetic enterprise is 1 Peter 3:15: "Always be prepared to give an answer *[apologia]* to everyone who asks you to give the reason for the hope that you have." Why, then, don't apologists examine Peter's own apologetic patterns and arguments (for example, in Acts) rather than leap only to a few Pauline texts (often out of context!) or, worse, a rationalistic philosophical basis? These are just three sample topics; the same could be said for violence, taxation, economics, biblical interpretation, eschatology, church leadership, mission and many other issues and areas.

In addition to James D. G. Dunn, at least two other ranking New Testament scholars have suggested the importance of a focus on Peter. Oscar Cullmann contends that Peter "certainly possesses a much greater significance in the foundation of Christian theology than we are accustomed to assume." "Theologically . . . scholars seem to me to be unjust to Peter when they put him entirely in the shadow of Paul, or regard him as Paul's antagonist devoid of understanding for the great Pauline insights."[11] And F. F. Bruce recently confessed rather candidly: "A Paulinist (and I myself must be so described) is under a constant temptation to underestimate Peter." Bruce goes on to say that more recently he has been moved (by Dunn's argument) "to think more highly of Peter's contribution to the early church."[12]

So the promise of Peter exists, but it remains largely unclaimed. Over the centuries, the Roman Catholic church has, of course, held that Peter was the chief of the apostles and has made a great deal of his importance. In Saint Peter's Basilica at the Vatican, for example, one can view a glittering "Chair of Saint Peter," the alleged tomb of Saint Peter under the awesome Bernini canopy and a famous thirteenth-century statue of Peter by Arnolfo di Cambio, whose bronze feet have been worn smooth by the kisses of millions of pilgrims eager to pay tribute to the great apostle. But while the greatness of the art and the sincere faith of many pilgrims are admirable, this mythologization of Peter obscures the very reasons he ought to be significant for the church today. it is not because Peter was the first pope speaking infallibly in imperial splendor (if this is what we imagine) that he is worthy of our attention. Rather, it is precisely because he was fallible, weak, sometimes knocked down but always getting up to resume the

Christian pilgrimage, that he holds special promise for those of us who give him the honor of our attention.

But Protestants have done no better. Perhaps partly in reaction to Catholicism, Protestants have tended (as F. F. Bruce says) to become "Paulinists." They have not mythologized Peter; they have just ignored him. But in so doing, Protestants are implicitly denying the authority of their rule of faith, Scripture, in which he looms so large and significant.

To this generally negative assessment, there have been exceptions of course. There are a few older "devotional" studies of Peter more or less along the lines of this book.[13] And in recent decades a handful of scholarly monographs (or parts of them) have looked more specifically at Peter.[14] But the threefold promise of Peter discussed above remains largely unclaimed. The older "devotional" studies, fine as they were in their day, are now rather distant from the contemporary situation in which we must make our application. The more scholarly studies, helpful as they are in some technical domains, tend to be preoccupied either with identifying (without much resolution) thorny textual and historical problems or with tedious arguments relative to the claims that Peter died in Rome, was the first bishop of Rome and universal head of Christ's church, and so on.

Sources and Method

What follows, then, is a study of New Testament Christianity and explorations of its contemporary meaning and application. It is pursued by trailing Peter through the New Testament in roughly chronological sequence and in topical fashion. To most closely approximate the path by which these chapters emerged, you should (1) read the biblical texts whose references stand at the head of each chapter; (2) observe and reflect on the aspects or sectors of our contemporary experience that might be addressed by God in this part of his Word; (3) return to the biblical texts for a more careful and intense study of what happened, what was said and why; this means examining not only various passages in the Gospels and Acts but also subsequent comments germane to the topic from Peter's Letters; (4) apply God's Word, as you understand it, to the present context as rigorously as possible. This process cannot be adequate, of course, if it is viewed too mechanically or individualistically. Repetition of the four movements above, consulting other writings, discussions with others, and prayer for God's assistance are also part of the process.

What this process amounts to, of course, is a kind of "dialectic" back and forth between the ancient biblical text and the modern world in which we live. Though there is necessarily and unavoidably an influence from our modern context on what we see and hear in Scripture, our effort must be to allow the Bible to speak both freely and authoritatively. In my text or footnotes some attention will be given to critical and interpretive problems that exist, along with some justification for my proposed resolution. Certain general starting points and procedures for these studies, however, can be briefly stated here.

First, the sources that we shall work with are the books of the New Testament. Peter is prominently mentioned in all four Gospels, the Acts, his two letters, and also in 1 Corinthians and Galatians. That these documents are not simple works of history, that there are differences of content and style, and that there are interpretive difficulties and frustrating silences must be noted—but these need not deter us from pursuing a study of Peter in the New Testament. That there are four distinctive Gospels (not one "harmonized" version) implies that our first and primary studies of Peter should be within these original literary contexts.

Nonetheless, there is justification for a look at a "composite portrait" of Peter in the New Testament. The fact is that there was *one Peter* (not four) behind the Gospel stories (and Acts, and the other literature). There are difficulties but in general outline the fuller composite portrait makes sense and rings true. Recall also that the early church was not made up of liars or imbeciles, and we may trust their judgment in drawing together the documents we have into *one collection* of reliable and true material—and their judgment to exclude various apocryphal works allegedly about or by Peter. Christians also have confidence that there is *one God* speaking his true Word through these diverse authors and settings. The New Testament thus invites the kind of study we undertake here. For scholars to wring their hands when we draw together the accounts in the four Gospels to form a composite account of what happened in the upper room before Jesus was betrayed, seems to me to be a manifestation of fear, negativism, hypercriticism and conservatism. This sort of distrust of God, the church and common sense is hardly appropriate when one is tracking Simon "Can-I-walk-on-the-water-Lord?" Peter!

Second, in reconstructing my portrait of Peter I will take courage and suggest certain possibilities in the interest of completing an explanation of a given incident or period. For example, I suggest why I think Jesus walked on the water; why Peter, James and John were the "inner circle"; why the disciples put down the nets at the suggestion of an unrecognized stranger on the shore; and what I think Peter did between A.D. 46-65. I make these suggestions respectfully (lots of "perhaps" and "maybe" language!) but hopefully, and I think carefully, in the interest of better grasping what happened in a realistic and helpful way.

Third, my interpretation and contemporary application of the Peter material needs some explanation. My question ultimately is this: "What might God be trying to say to us today in this material?" Matthew's purpose in reporting Jesus' walk on the water may have been to help authenticate his deity by a nature miracle. Fine and important. But my interpretation and application of Jesus' and then Peter's walk on the water is provoked by Jesus' statement, concluding this story, about the problem of faith. I am much less interested in the mechanics of walking on water or its uniqueness than I am in the ongoing and contemporary importance of how faith must be expressed in risking what appears to be impossible at the call of Christ. So with all the great healing stories. I am less concerned with the spectacular, instantaneous nature of most of these than I am with (a) the fact that sick people are helped to become well, and (b) their healing comes at the command and by the power of Jesus Christ. In short, I reject the idea that these and other events are so inextricably bound up with a particular and spectacular *modus operandi* that they now exist *only* as signs of Christ's deity with no relevance for our discipleship. I do not propose an allegorical interpretation but rather an "essentialist" or "thematic" interpretation of these events, applying this perspective, then, to our situation.

Fourth, and finally, in assessing the contemporary scene, especially in the church, I seek honesty and courageous self-criticism. But, as I hope is clear in the discussions, the criticism is directed at myself and my communities as much as any others. But my point is never finally negative. We need to invite God to question us and correct us. It is painful to be confronted by the Lord and to have to repent. But Peter teaches us that this part of Christian discipleship leads to growth and true victory. As I hope we will see, such a process is infinitely better than a life of comfortable delusion.

For Reflection or Discussion

1. What has been your previous image of Peter (if you have thought or heard about him)? What stories about him have impressed you most in the past?

2. Who are some of your most important "heroes" or "models" for your life (biblical or nonbiblical, ancient or recent)? What is it about these "models" that you find attractive or helpful?

3. Is it helpful or harmful to know about the weaknesses, failures or defeats of such models? Why do you think the biblical figures are so often depicted in their failures as well as victories (for example, Moses, David)?

2 Beginnings: The Meaning of Conversion

"Follow me."

CONVERSION, AS A GENERAL PHENOMENON, HAS LONG BEEN A TOPIC OF great interest not only to religious people but to psychologists, sociologists, business entrepreneurs and political leaders. What is it that causes a sometimes radical change of allegiance and personality? The converters and the converted may rejoice, but family and friends often worry about the convert. In some cases they may even call in a psychologist or "deprogrammer" in an effort to reverse the conversion. Short of such drastic measures there is still good reason to take a careful, critical look at the means and results of this process. Techniques of persuasion and propaganda have been honed to such levels of effectiveness that, given the right circumstances, almost any person can be conditioned to think and act in any fashion. The advertising industry knows this well.

But how is it that people become Christians, followers of Jesus Christ? To use the traditional, biblical terms, how is it that people are *saved, born again* and *converted?* For those who are born into Christian families and raised in churches this is often an odd question. Whether baptized or "dedicated" as infants in the Christian milieu or not, it is hard for a large percentage of Christians to recall a time when they were *not* living in relation to Jesus Christ as Savior, Lord and God! Yet even in these cases, parents and church leaders usually stress the importance of a thoughtful, conscious decision to "accept Christ personally" and "join the church" at some stage. Often this decision is pressed in adolescence—whether in the form of a particular prayer, a public testimony, a baptism, or a ceremony concluding catechism or confirmation studies. Minimally, adult Christians who have "always" been part of the church are choosing "with their feet" to continue this association, even though in most places in the world they are quite free to leave. But what is this choice—and why make it?

Another large group of Christians is not composed of "second-generation" disciples but of people from many different backgrounds who have very consciously made a decision to change from some kind of non-Christian to some kind of Christian. According to the professional pollsters there has been a remarkable numerical resurgence of Christianity in our generation, not least in the United States. For some of these people, conversion occurred when they walked forward at a Billy Graham crusade as the mass choir sang "Just As I Am." Others phoned in to affirm their decision to convert to Christ when they listened to an impassioned plea by a "televangelist" like Jim Bakker, Pat Robertson or Jimmy Swaggart. Others concluded Bible studies or presentations of summaries of the gospel like the "Four Spiritual Laws" by praying with a Christian to receive Christ. Some converts are frightened by the terrors of death into praying with a door-to-door evangelist. Some are moved to conversion by the promise of an abundant and successful life as they hear various Christian "stars" give their story. Some converts are convinced to become Christians by logical arguments (C. S. Lewis was one). Others are converted after reading the Bible by themselves (Jacques Ellul, for example).

So the circumstances, reasons, language and concepts of Christian conversion vary a great deal today. The importance of re-examining Christian conversion lies partly in the fact that many non-Christians are searching for a framework that gives meaning to their lives and are open to the possibility of becoming Christians. And, on the other hand, people who are already Christians are often highly motivated to seek to bring others to Jesus Christ. This is partly because they wish to share God's good gift of life with others. And it is partly because their own leader, Jesus, commanded them to engage in mission and evangelism: "Go and make disciples of all nations" (Mt 28:19). Christians sometimes feel as passionate about this as Paul: "I have become all things to all [people] so that by all possible means I might save some" (1 Cor 9:22).

It is in these circumstances that we need to go back to the New Testament and clearly observe what is involved in conversion, in one's becoming a follower of Jesus Christ. A careful look at Peter's experience and his view of conversion is a promising avenue to take. As it turned out, he was not only one of the very first converts to Christianity, but one of its most significant. Peter experienced conversion, he preached it to non-Christians and he taught about it to Christian churches.

First Encounter (Jn 1:35-42)
Whether out of simple curiosity, political interest, personal meaninglessness or some other motive, two members of Peter's fishing business began to spend time listening to a strange, charismatic prophet giving speeches in their area. Both Andrew (Simon Peter's brother) and John (brother of James and son of Zebedee) quickly became disciples of John the Baptist. The Baptist's two-pronged message was simple and powerful: First, what is wrong with the world is human sin and perversity, so "repent" of your sin and symbolize this repudiation by being publicly dipped (baptized) in water. Second, the answer to our situation is coming soon. Get ready to meet the Messiah, the promised one of Israel! Who knows what Peter, James and the others back at the fishing docks thought, whether they were amused, worried, curious or patronizing. Perhaps they had some long, stormy conversations as they all worked or sat around the house together.

The day came soon (within a few weeks or months) when at last John the Baptist positively identified Jesus of Nazareth, the carpenter, as the Messiah, the "Lamb of God who takes away the sin of the world." Andrew and John lost no time in approaching Jesus and asking him where he lived. During the day they spent together with Jesus, at his invitation, they found out a great deal more about him and he, undoubtedly, found out more about them, their families and business. Andrew and John left this remarkable encounter convinced that John the Baptist was correct.

Andrew went back to Simon (and John to James) with a simple but enthusiastic message and an equally simple objective. "We have found the Messiah!" was the message Andrew brought to Simon. The objective was to bring Simon to meet Jesus personally. John reports that when Jesus met Simon for the first time he said simply, "You are Simon son of John. You will be called Cephas [the Rock or Peter]" (Jn 1:42). Quite possibly there was more said than just this, unless many people were crowding around Jesus at the time. But this is the gist of what happened. End of first encounter.

Decision Day (Mt 4:18-22; Mk 1:16-20; Lk 5:1-11)

In the several weeks which followed this first encounter, Simon had a lot to think about. Who is this man? What did he mean that I will be called "the Rock"? Perhaps Simon heard more about Jesus through Andrew or others—stories about his alleged birth to a virgin, reports of genealogical records linking Jesus to the royal family of David, speculations of how his appearance corresponded to predictions cryptically made by the ancient prophets, stories of a confrontation with Satan in the wilderness, of powerful preaching and miraculous healing, of his rejection by the religious experts and leaders of his hometown, Nazareth. Perhaps! Minimally, Simon saw and heard Jesus again occasionally in the coming weeks in and around Bethsaida and Capernaum. Jesus was attracting a lot of attention in their neighborhood. Possibly, Jesus visited Simon's and Andrew's house.

Decision day in Simon's conversion experience came rather suddenly and surprisingly. Mark (1:16-20) and Matthew (4:18-22) give the story in very short form. Luke (5:1-11) gives the more detailed version to which we turn. Simon and company had finished fishing for the day—not a very good catch as it happened. Simon and Andrew were cleaning up their equipment. Nearby, John and James were mending some holes in their nets. Suddenly a crowd began to gather near their boats. As Simon looked up, he saw that it was Jesus—the people had found him walking along the beach and now pressed him to give a talk. They wanted to hear "the word of God." Jesus agreed and, in order to be better seen and heard, got into Simon's boat to use it as a platform.

When he finished his talk, Jesus turned to Simon and gave the startling advice, "Put out into deep water, and let down the nets for a catch." Simon's first reaction, as a veteran fisherman talking to a carpenter after an unsuccessful morning already, with the nets cleaned and put away, was to respectfully disagree: "Master, we've worked hard all night and haven't caught anything." On second thought, however, he agreed: "But because you say so, I will let down the nets." When they did this, the catch was so huge the nets began to break, and they had to call their partners over to help bring it in. The boats were quickly filled and began to sink deeper into the water. A miracle had occurred in their lives.

Simon's stunned reaction to this event was to fall at Jesus' knees and say, "Go away from me, Lord; I am a sinful man!" Jesus quickly replied, "Don't be afraid; from now on you will catch [people]." Or as Mark and Matthew phrase it: "Follow me, and I will make you fishers of [people]." Immediately, Simon (with Andrew, James and John, to whom the invitation also came) tied up the boats, left everything in the charge of Zebedee and the hired hands and followed Jesus.

What we have in these two episodes is the story of Simon Peter's conversion. Before them he is not a follower of Jesus; after them he has embarked on a new life as a disciple. How are we to assess the first encounter? Peter followed his brother to meet Jesus, heard him say a few words and returned home without making any commitments. No conversion can be chalked up but neither should it be regarded as a failure or waste of time. This first encounter was an important incident which set the stage for the day of decision later on. For those thinking about becoming Christians (and for those who are engaged in trying to win converts to Jesus Christ), Peter's experience is an important model in several ways.

What is impressive about Simon, first of all, is his *openness*. With an open mind he hears out Andrew and then Jesus. He listens to them. He is willing to consider the possibilities. He does not prematurely close up to the strange new talk from his brother about finding the Messiah. Of course the encounter concludes as openly as it began; no commitments or even statements by Simon are reported.

Second, Peter is not merely "open" but willing to actively *investigate* the situation. He gets up and goes with Andrew to meet Jesus. He makes the effort to learn more; he is not just open "in theory."

Third, his investigation is centered on the *person* of Jesus. He does not just investigate various ideas about Messianic prophecy or religion—he goes to meet and learn more about Jesus himself. The investigation focuses on who Jesus is, or might be. It is important to note that Andrew's message was a simple declaration about this man: " 'We have found the Messiah' (that is, the Christ)." Similarly, John the Baptist said, "Look, the Lamb of God who takes away the sin of the world!" (Jn 1:29). In the same chapter of John's Gospel, Philip tells Nathaniel, "We have found the one Moses wrote about in the Law, and about whom the prophets also wrote" (v. 45). Christianity is about a person, Jesus Christ; everything else is secondary.

In short, Peter's first encounter is an open-minded investigation of the person of Jesus Christ. For Peter, and I think for everyone who adopts this approach, such an encounter becomes an event of hope and promise. Peter looks for Jesus with his brother, and he finds him. He hears Jesus say to him "You are Simon . . . you will be called the Rock!" Peter discovers in his investigation that Jesus is not first of all a threat to him but a promise. You *are* . . . but you *will be*. Perhaps Andrew (or John) had told Jesus about Peter's intensity, strength, boldness—and instability. In any event, Peter's first discovery of Jesus was that he is a man of hope and promise.

First encounters: open, personal, hopeful, intriguing, positive. If we have such encounters with Jesus Christ—or if we help bring them about for others—well and good. Still, we find a specific day of crisis and decision in Simon's developing relationship with Jesus. Christian conversion is both a *moment* and a *process*. Simon was beginning to change from the first encounter he had with Jesus. One cannot truly see Jesus without being affected in some way. And even after the moment of decision, the process of converting from one set of loyalties, one style of life to another continues throughout one's life. But there is a crisis, a specific time of decision. "Prenatal" spiritual life is real but still hidden and uncertain. There comes a moment of birth.

As we did with the first encounter, let us observe carefully Simon's decisive moment of conversion. First, it is provoked by and centered on the person of *Jesus Christ*—not an organization, a set of doctrines or anything else. It has to do with joining Jesus (not an organization), believing in Jesus (not just believing certain ideas).

This Jesus speaks and acts. It is the Word of God and the mighty acts of God in Jesus Christ that provoke the conversion. Jesus teaches from the boat, advises Simon to let down his nets, causes the miracle to occur, calls Simon to follow him. Note also that there is both a public and a personal aspect to the action of the Word of God in Jesus Christ. On the one hand, there are people around and Jesus addresses the crowd. So too, Simon's decision to follow Jesus is made in full view of these people: it is a public, not private, conversion. But on the other hand, Jesus individualizes his words and actions. He invades Simon's boat, works in Simon's business in its ordinary surroundings and speaks a challenge directly to this individual. Simon responds as an individual directly to this Jesus.

These observations ought to encourage us today not to view Christianity so much in "religious" terms. It is in daily life, in my neighborhood, in my work, that Jesus will meet me. Jesus is not necessarily most clearly and decisively encountered in an atmosphere of robes, choirs, liturgies or the ecstasy of pentecostal worship! By no means is he absent there either, but fundamentally Christianity is an affair of daily life more than of religious gatherings. What is Jesus saying and doing today in political and economic life, in your family and neighborhood, in your personal existence? Simon's story gives us reason to look for him there.

Second, consider two aspects of *Simon's response* to this intervention of Jesus Christ, both of which are essential in authentic conversion. The first is *repentance;* the second is *faith.* Repentance is the no which we pronounce to our own "lordship" of our life. Fundamentally, sin is the choice to serve ourself rather than God, to worship the creature rather than the Creator. All specific sins (murder, theft, adultery, injustice and so on) are variations on this theme, manifestations of this more basic problem. While sin and repentance do not arise in Simon's first encounter with Jesus, eventually they must be confronted.

Simon's repentance is reflected in both his words and his actions. Genuine repentance is never just a matter of "saying you're sorry" or making only a verbal repudiation of your sin. Words must be accompanied by deeds. Simon's repentance is demonstrated in his refusal of his own inclination to hang up the nets for the day, by his explicit confession "I am a sinful man," and by his "leaving all" to follow Jesus. Note once again that this repentance is precipitated by the presence of Jesus in his holiness and power. It is not beaten into Simon or cajoled out of him. The best way to insure deep and genuine repentance is to have a clear, personal encounter with Jesus Christ.

But repentance is only one side of Simon's response. The other side is faith, the yes Simon expresses in word and action to Jesus. Faith means trust and commitment. It is partly intellectual ("believing that" Jesus is the Lord and Christ) but equally a volitional commitment of one's life ("believing *on*" Jesus). Simon's faith is expressed by obedience to Jesus' command to let down the nets again, by his falling to his knees and calling Jesus "Lord," and by his following Jesus. Note well that Simon performs no "good works" in order to be acceptable as a follower of Jesus. He does nothing to earn his salvation. At the same time, it is a terrible error to think that faith (any more than repentance) is genuine when unexpressed in action. The great German pastor Dietrich Bonhoeffer, more than any other recent figure, called attention to the heresy of "cheap grace," that is grace without repentance, grace without discipleship.[1] We human beings are composites of intellect, will and feelings in a physical frame. Both repentance and faith are expressed in all of these dimensions of our daily life.

Finally, *Jesus' response to Simon* is to *accept him* in his repentance. He accepts Simon as he is and removes his fear: "Do not be afraid." Simultaneously Jesus provides a *challenge* and a promise: "Follow me and I will make you a fisher of [people]." It is a difficult challenge to begin a new life of following Jesus but it is a real possibility and a promise. We *can* live this kind of life. Jesus is not a monarch issuing orders from some imperial throne. He is the Servant Lord who promises to walk with us, leading us and accompanying us at all times.

If in the first encounter Jesus brought Simon a hopeful promise of what he would *be* (the Rock), in this second episode he brings him a hopeful promise of what he will *do* ("fish" for people). Simon will find and "capture alive" people for the way, the truth and the life. Again, Jesus brings his hope and promise into Simon's real life and circumstances. This fisherman is going to do some "fishing" on a level, with a meaning and purpose, he never could have dreamed of before. Jesus means hope and promise!

One frequent misunderstanding also deserves our attention before leaving this story. We read that they left everything and followed Jesus. Later on Jesus said things such as the following: "If anyone comes to me and does not hate his father and mother, his wife and children, his brothers and sisters—yes, even his own life—he cannot be my disciple" (Lk 14:26). How could the greatest advocate and exemplar of love in history have meant what this text (and others like it) appears to say? It is a superficial interpretation to think that Jesus was issuing this extremely radical call simply for an initial band of monks taking vows of poverty and celibacy. Rather, Jesus was speaking hyperbolically (in extreme dialectical fashion) to express the *absolute priority* of the kingdom of God over all other claims on our lives. The famous text in the Sermon on the Mount summarizes this well: "Seek first his kingdom and his righteousness, and all these things will be given to you as well" (Mt 6:33).

So Simon "left everything" and followed Jesus. It was a decisive change of direction and loyalty. And yet, *at the very same time* his brother Andrew and their fishing partners and buddies, James and John, do the same thing. The call to conversion must be heard and accepted individually, but it brings us into a community. It is individual but not individualistic. In similar fashion we find Peter's wife going with him on speaking tours later on, we find him concerned about his mother-in-law's health, and we find him fishing again. He has not joined a monastic order! He had joined the new community led by the Lord of everyday life.

Second Thoughts about Conversion (1 Peter)

How did Peter look at the subject of conversion thirty-five years later? It is interesting to recall (see chapter one) that in the same period of two or three years in Rome in the early sixties Peter was probably giving Mark material for his Gospel and writing his own first Letter. In this letter the familiar themes of repentance and faith are continued. The absolute centrality of the person of Jesus Christ is maintained. The theme of hope and promise dominates Peter's discussion of conversion. But there are some additional observations that he wishes to make about the process.

Like his partner John (Jn 3), Peter finds it helpful to describe conversion as being "born again" (1 Pet 1:3, 23; 2:2). On the one hand, this imagery is helpful in depicting the decisive new life which commences at conversion to Jesus Christ. A whole new way of life begins. On the other hand, the image of being "born again" suggests that the origin of our life is in a parent and not in ourselves. When we *experience* the call to conversion, it is a call to decision and action on our part. When we *reflect* on it later, we are usually impressed by how little credit we can take for it! It is a gracious action of God's power and love in giving us new life. So in Peter's first letter he stresses the active participation of the Trinity: God the Father has "chosen" us and in his "great mercy" he has "given us" this new birth (1 Pet 1:1-3). So too God's Holy Spirit is active in the preaching of the gospel and in sanctifying those who are converted (1 Pet 1:2, 12).

As for the Son of God, Peter slowly came to realize that Jesus was not only the Christ (Messiah) but also the "Lamb of God," as John the Baptist had said. It was necessary for Jesus to suffer and die. Thus, in his letter Peter wrote some of the most powerful and illuminating sentences in the New Testament with regard to this aspect of Jesus and conversion. We have been redeemed "with the precious blood of Christ, a lamb without blemish or defect" (1 Pet 1:19). "He himself bore our sins in his body on the tree, so that we might die to sins and live for righteousness; by his wounds you have been healed" (1 Pet 2:24). And finally, "Christ died for sins once for all, the righteous for the unrighteous, to bring you to God. He was put to death in the body but made alive by the Spirit" (1 Pet 3:18).[2]

With respect to hope, Peter's perspective was enlarged by the time of his first letter. He continued to stress that those who know Christ "are receiving the goal of [their] faith" (1 Pet 1:9), and that the Christian newborn has a whole lifetime of growing up ahead of him or her (1 Pet 2:2). But his hope is now anchored in the promise of a final eschatological fulfillment, in the coming of Jesus Christ and the kingdom of God at the end of "ordinary" history. Just as Jesus Christ entered this fulfillment after his resurrection from the dead, so shall his followers. "He has given us new birth into a living hope through the resurrection of Jesus Christ from the dead, and into an inheritance that can never perish, spoil or fade—kept in heaven for you" (1 Pet 1:3-4). Peter's concept of the hope of Christian conversion has not become "otherworldly" as opposed to "this worldly." Rather, it is "both worldly."

As we approach the meaning of conversion and the beginnings of the Christian life today, we should retain this larger perspective given in Peter's letter, along with that of the Gospels. The Jesus we encounter in daily life is the one who died for our sins and was resurrected for our justification. He is the one who came to earth, and he is the one who will return. At the same time, the basic meaning of conversion, the basic movement, remains what we have observed in the conversion of Simon Peter: a personal encounter with Jesus in our ordinary existence, repentance from our sin, a commitment of our life in faith to Jesus as Lord, and the taking of the first faltering, uncertain steps of following him.

For Reflection or Discussion

1. How would you describe your "first encounter" with Jesus Christ? What were the circumstances? How did you react then? How do you look at it now?
2. If you are a Christian, how would you describe your conversion? What were the circumstances? How has your mind changed about conversion, Jesus Christ and the Christian life since your conversion?
3. Do you think it is helpful to develop a "formula" for presenting the gospel to others? If so, what elements need to be included, and how would you express them? If not, how would you share the gospel with a non-Christian?

I Conversion

II Discipleship
    (A) Draw near to God +
            His community
    (B) Preach Gospel of Christ
    (C) Healing + cast out demons

3 Three Tasks: The Content of Discipleship

"Calling the Twelve to him,
he sent them out two by two."

CONVERSION IS JUST THE BEGINNING OF THE CHRISTIAN LIFE, THE FIRST step in following Jesus Christ. There is something pathetic about the kind of Christianity that stresses conversion so heavily that there is little room for anything else. Churches (and individuals) with eyes only for conversion are the spiritual counterparts of those for whom marriage means nothing except the production of more babies. It is as tragic as if a person spent his or her life doing nothing but looking at albums of baby pictures. No doubt conversion, being "born again," is a great and stunning miracle! But it is just the beginning.

What does it mean to live a Christian life? How does the spiritual newborn grow up? What happens when we "leave all and follow" Jesus? In the briefest possible description, the Christian life is one of *discipleship*. The Greek word for "disciple" *(mathetes)* is used some two hundred and seventy times in the Gospels and Acts. It means "learner." It implies practice as well as intellectual formation. That is, the disciple does not just have certain ideas and opinions; he or she behaves in certain ways, living out those ideas. The Christian disciple is one trained and taught by Jesus Christ, one who "follows after" Jesus.

One attractive distortion of the meaning of the Christian life is the notion that faithful discipleship is essentially a matter of holding the correct ideas, beliefs and doctrines. On this understanding, the person who affirms, for example, the premillennial rapture of the saints, or the inerrancy of the original autographs of the Bible, or the creation of the world during six days six thousand years ago, or any number of other doctrinal possibilities, is qualified as a faithful, genuine disciple. Any Christian holding variant views on these issues is judged a defective disciple. It may even be that some church or conference will ban or condemn a pious, humble man or woman of God who happens to hold a different interpretation of some doctrine on one day, but on the next roll out the red carpet for some guru with whose ideas and doctrines they agree but whose behavioral record (such as marriage or financial dealings) is better left unmentioned!

An opposite but equally attractive distortion of the meaning of Christian discipleship is to make everything depend on certain behavior or practices. In this "revised version" of discipleship, one is an authentic disciple if he or she dresses or wears the hair in certain ways, uses certain language in public prayers, attends the "right" church regularly, lights candles, takes mass or celebrates the Lord's Supper frequently, belongs to lots of church committees, lives simply, joins an intentional community, gives a lot of money to the church, or is arrested in nonviolent demonstrations. Virtually any opinion or doctrine may be held (but keep it quiet, if possible!) so long as one's behavior is observably "correct" by one of these standards.

Even if we repudiate the preceding extremes and adopt a more wholistic, biblical emphasis on the mutual importance of faith and works, doctrine and practice, inward belief and outward behavior, we may still face the problem of locating the center. It is essential that this center be Jesus Christ. It is, to give two examples, a misappropriation of Paul to center on him, and it is a misappropriation of the Holy Spirit to center everything on the doctrine and experience of the Spirit. Why? Because Paul continually points away from himself to Christ. Because the role of the Spirit is to "testify about" and "remind us of" none other than Jesus Christ (see Jn 14:26; 15:26). Christian discipleship means following Jesus Christ. What did that entail for Simon Peter as he began following Jesus? What does it imply for our understanding of discipleship today?

Three Tasks in a Resistant World

Not long after Simon's conversion, Jesus formally chose twelve disciples. He "called to him those he wanted, and they came to him. He appointed twelve . . . that they might be with him and that he might send them out to preach and to have authority to drive out demons" (Mk 3:13-15). In parallel and similar texts we discover that the twelve were sent out to preach the "kingdom of God" (Lk 9:2) and that they were sent out in pairs—"two by two" (Mk 6:7). So, too, "authority to drive out evil spirits" (exorcism) was elaborated in terms of healing "every disease and sickness" (Mt 10:1; see Lk 9:1-2). For the first official band of Christian disciples, their "job description" had these three elements: (1) being with Jesus in his community, (2) proclaiming the kingdom of God, and (3) ridding people of domination of evil spirits and disabling injury or disease. With Jesus, the Twelve (chosen in analogy with the original twelve patriarchs with whom God founded his work with Israel) were the founders and exemplars of a new way of life with God in the world.

Before examining each of the three tasks of discipleship in turn, let me be clear about the basic thrust. I believe that this threefold agenda for the original twelve disciples is, when adequately interpreted, the calling of all disciples of Jesus in every place and time. Here's why.

First of all, a Christian is a follower of Jesus Christ. Jesus is our model and pattern in a very important sense. It is precisely these three tasks that characterized the life of Jesus in the world. If you read the Gospels and jot down a simple list of what Jesus spent his time doing, these three items would head the list. He drew near to God and to his followers in the community of faith, he preached the kingdom of God, and he healed people and combatted the demonic powers.

Recall Simon Peter's first experiences of Jesus: (1) He hears Jesus proclaim the good news, (2) he is called to follow, to join Jesus and be with him[1] and (3) either just before his conversion (according to Luke) or just after (Matthew and Mark), Peter sees Jesus enter his house and heal his sick mother-in-law. She lay ill with a high fever and Jesus "took her hand and helped her up." He "rebuked the fever and it left her" (Mk 1:31; Lk 4:39). This was not just *Peter's* experience of Jesus! If we were to outline the first chapter of Mark or the fourth chapter of Matthew, we would find that these three tasks are the work of Jesus from the beginning. And they are his work to the end—even his death and resurrection expressed and fulfilled these three tasks.

So if Jesus' example is our guide, that is the first reason to make this agenda our own. Second, however, he also specifically commissioned or commanded his twelve disciples to carry out this threefold agenda (as we have seen earlier). If Peter and his colleagues are models of "followers of Christ"—as I think they are—this command by Jesus has to be taken seriously with respect to *our* discipleship. That this agenda was not limited to the Twelve is also clear in that later the Seventy (symbolically representing God's universal purposes, because it was thought there were seventy nations in the world) went out with the same tasks (see Lk 10:1-20). That the agenda is not limited to the earthly, pre-Pentecost ministry of Jesus and the Twelve (or Seventy) is clear when we turn to Acts. The post-Pentecost church carried out the same threefold agenda: building the community of God in Jesus Christ, proclaiming the good news of God's rule, and healing those sick and oppressed by the principalities and powers.

That is the basic argument and rationale. We turn now to the specifics.

Cultivating a Life with Jesus Christ: The First Task

"Follow me!" Jesus chose the twelve "to be with him." Christian discipleship is first and foremost a life with Jesus Christ. Although I have described this as one of three tasks, it is important to stress that this is more a matter of *being* than it is *doing*, more a relationship than an agenda. Throughout the earthly ministry of Jesus of Nazareth, he cultivated and built up this group of brothers and sisters. He wanted them around during times of feasting and celebration (Mt 11:19; Jn 2) and later in a time of deep distress he would still say, "I have eagerly desired to eat this Passover with you before I suffer" (Lk 22:15). Jesus said to his disciples, "You are those who have stood by me in my trials" and promised a future time when "you may eat and drink at my table in my kingdom" (Lk 22:28-30). Having his disciples close to himself was Jesus' promise for the future: "I will come back and take you to be with me that you also may be where I am" (Jn 14:3). It was his promise for the ongoing present: "Where two or three come together in my name, there am I with them" (Mt 18:20). "Surely I will be with you always, to the very end of the age" (Mt 28:20).

In the person of Jesus we recognize the perfect "God-for-man"; that is, God is fully present in Jesus Christ as he draws close to men and women. Simultaneously, however, we may see in Jesus the perfect "man-for-God." Thus, Jesus demonstrates throughout his life a determination to spend time with God the Father in prayer and meditation (Mt 14:23; Mk 1:35; Lk 6:12). His only desire is to know and perform the will of God the Father (Mk 14:36; Jn 17). In fact, Jesus can say "I and my Father are one" and pray that his disciples may be similarly united with each other and with him (Jn 17:22-23). Jesus is simultaneously the model of one who is wholly "for God" and "with God"— and the model of God incarnate who is seeking followers to be "for" and "with" him.

None of this comes as any surprise to those familiar with the Old Testament. In the creation, Adam and Eve are created to live in unimpeded relationship with God (Gen 1—2). The great rebellion, the fall into sin, leads directly to an interruption of their personal relationship with God. They "hide" from God (Gen 3:8). God's first question for them is, "Where are you?" (v. 9). As in Peter's conversion episode ("Go away from me, Lord; I am a sinful man") there is an instinctive fleeing and hiding from God which follows from our sin and fear of encountering the Holy One. Cain also left the presence of the Lord after his murder of Abel (Gen 4:16).

Over and over God said to Israel, "I will be your God and you will be my people" (Deut 7:6). The prophet Isaiah phrased God's feelings as follows: "My chosen . . . I formed for myself that they may proclaim my praise" (Is 43:20-21). The Psalms continually stress the theme of being "with God": "You will fill me with joy in your presence, with eternal pleasures at your right hand" (Ps 16:11). "As the deer pants for streams of water, so my soul pants for you, O God. My soul thirsts for God, for the living God. When can I go and meet with God?" (Ps 42:1-2).

Discipleship means being with Jesus Christ, developing a living relationship with God. What did this mean concretely for Peter and his friends? It meant the whole gamut of interpersonal experience: eating and drinking, traveling, working and celebrating, resting and struggling, quiet observation and thought, active conversation. Conversation is, perhaps, the critical ingredient. Without a two-way conversation there can be little growth in a personal relationship of any kind. It means talking, asking questions, making statements. It means listening. A great deal of the New Testament record of Peter, Jesus and company is a report of such conversation.

Today when we read or hear Scripture with an open, attentive eagerness to understand not only what is being said but also "what is God trying to say to me?" we are listening to the same Word of God Peter encountered in Jesus Christ. When we bring our questions to the Word of God, our requests to God in prayer, when we compliment, praise and thank God in our prayers, songs and other statements, we are conversing with the same Jesus Christ Peter talked to, the same God David addressed in his great psalm. Conversation with God is still possible and it is still essential in carrying out this first dimension of discipleship, being with God.

Being with God has both an individual and a group dimension. Sometimes Jesus and the disciples interacted as a whole group; other times it was Jesus and Peter, one-to-one. In our own era the same two dimensions remain important. Discipleship means cultivating a personal, individual life of prayer, meditation and instruction in the Word of God. Equally essential is the cultivation of a corporate relationship to other Christian brothers and sisters and to God. We will return to this latter matter (the church) in chapter four.

There are certain results from cultivating a relationship with God in Jesus Christ. Our character is remolded, our prayers and questions are often answered, our spirits are lifted, our minds learn wonderful new things. By this kind of association with Christ we grow. Thirty-five years after his own spiritual rebirth, Peter urged his fellow disciples: "Like newborn babies, crave pure spiritual milk, so that by it you may grow up in your salvation, now that you have tasted that the Lord is good" (1 Pet 2:2-3). And in a famous statement Peter advises: "Cast all your anxiety on him because he cares for you" (1 Pet 5:7).

Associating with Jesus Christ, conversing with God, makes a difference. Mature Christian discipleship, however, means getting beyond a merely "utilitarian" view of the presence of Christ. This is no easy challenge! The world in which we live resists and contests the concept of an "unproductive," gratuitous relationship based solely on love. One of Jesus' temptations in the wilderness was precisely on this issue. Jesus was challenged to demonstrate that he could *use* God—exploit his power—by throwing himself off the pinnacle and then claiming God's promise of protection in Scripture (Mt 4:5-7)!

Maturing as a Christian disciple does not mean a lack of concern or appreciation for what God does in our life. It does not mean that we cease pleading with God to intervene in one context or another. But it does mean subordinating these things to a much broader and deeper relationship to God, in which we grow to know him, spend time with him, praise him and love him *simply* for who he is. So discipleship, first of all, means cultivating a life with the God we know in Jesus Christ—both in our individual existence and as members of Christ's community.

Proclaiming the Good News of God's Kingdom: the Second Task

There is a kind of priority of "being" over "doing" in Christian discipleship. Being "with Christ" is the hub, the center, out from which radiate the "spokes." The disciples are sent out two by two, but they come back for time with Jesus before going out again. But the relationship is one of priority, not exclusivity. Christian discipleship is not whole, not authentic, without the "doing." Christianity is not a "holy club." As noted earlier, there are two basic dimensions to the disciple's penetration of the world: proclaiming the good news of the kingdom of God and engaging in healing and exorcism. The first has primarily to do with our words; the second has primarily to do with our actions.

The proclamation of the gospel of the kingdom was absolutely central and explicit for John the Baptist (Mt 3:2), Jesus (Mk 1:15; Lk 4:43), the twelve disciples (Lk 9:2) and the seventy who were later sent out by Jesus with the same assignment (Lk 10:1-11). While the terminology of "kingdom" *(basilea)* is used most frequently in the synoptic Gospels (Matthew, Mark and Luke), it is also employed in John's Gospel, the Acts of the Apostles, Paul's Letters and the Apocalypse. Paul, in Rome at the close of the story of the Acts of the Apostles, "Boldly and without hindrance . . . preached the kingdom of God and taught about the Lord Jesus Christ" (Acts 28:31). It is plainly incorrect to suggest that the gospel of the kingdom is *replaced* by the gospel of the church after Pentecost. At the very same time Paul, Peter, John and others were writing their Letters, they and others were editing and writing down the four Gospels—and certainly not just as chronicles for the library archives! The Gospels and Letters were complementary documents, not rival or even successive conceptions. The letters augment and fill out the meaning of the Gospels. The church is a manifestation of the kingdom. Paul preached the gospel of the kingdom (Acts 28:20 and elsewhere), but he taught and wrote mostly about the church. Why? Because the Gospels were the appropriate place for the basic description of the kingdom by the King, Jesus Christ, in his sermons, parables and so on. Paul did not need to repeat what was a well-known stock of Jesus' stories and explanations—circulated first orally and in various written texts, then edited into our four Gospels.

While the terminology varies, even in the Old Testament there was a clear expectation of the coming of a Messiah, the true heir of David's throne.[2] The terminology varies in the New Testament also ("kingdom," "kingdom of God," "kingdom of heaven," "kingdom of Christ"). In John's most famous chapter, Jesus tells Nicodemus he must be "born again" in order to see the "kingdom of God." This is a clear parallel to his call (in the same context) to "believe in" God's Son for "eternal life" (Jn 3:3, 5, 15-16). The "kingdom of God" means "eternal life." I do not wish to deny nuances that may differentiate these terms. What I want to stress here is the larger commonality among all of these expressions.[3]

In essence, the kingdom of God is the *rule* of God. The gospel, the good news, is that this rule has arrived on our planet and may be known and accepted in Jesus Christ, the anointed King of this kingdom. If sin is fundamentally the choice to be ruled by the self, or by various petty gods and idols, salvation is the repudiation of these competitors in favor of allegiance to the true God. It is good news that one can transfer loyalty and citizenship from the realm of Satan to the realm of Jesus Christ. The rule of Satan means death, misery, oppression, violence, slavery and dehumanization—even if it is sometimes wrapped up in a slick, skillfully marketed package. The rule of God in Jesus Christ means freedom, hope, life, truth, forgiveness and love—even if the ambassadors of Jesus Christ sometimes fail to adequately communicate this.

In the Gospels Jesus told many parables to explain the character of this kingdom and the way it grows in the world. In the Sermon on the Mount and elsewhere, Jesus described the ethics of the kingdom, the impact this rule of God should have on all phases of daily life. In the "synoptic apocalypse" (Mt 24; Mk 13; Lk 21), Jesus described future aspects of the kingdom and its coming. In the trial and death of Jesus, the radical clash between the rule of God and the designs of Satan occurred. In the resurrection the triumph of the kingdom of God was demonstrated.

The most important distinction that must be noted is not between the "kingdom of God" and the "kingdom of heaven" or between any other terms. Rather, it is the distinction which cuts across all of these terms, between the *already* and the *not yet*. Thus, eternal life is a real, present possession (Jn 3:36) but will only be fully realized in the future (see Jn 14). On the one hand "the kingdom of God is within [or among] you" (Lk 17:20-21). On the other hand, just as sprouting leaves signal the coming of summer, "When you see [certain] things happening, you know that the kingdom of God is near" (Lk 21:29-31). Thus the rule of God is really here, really available in Jesus Christ. Yet it is not fully here, and will not be fully here, until the eschaton, the consummation of history and the Second Coming of Christ.

Peter would later explain that any delay in the arrival of the final consummation is a result of God's patience and love, not any forgetfulness or defeat (2 Pet 3:8ff.)! In both of his letters, Peter stressed the fact that Christian discipleship ought to be inspired and shaped by this coming kingdom (1 Pet 4:7ff.; 2 Pet 3:11ff.). Thus, while the kingdom is only partially here, it is nevertheless truly here. Where the King is, the kingdom is present. Proclaiming the kingdom means proclaiming the King, Jesus Christ, and his gracious rule as Lord.

We noted in the preceding discussion that there is a radical contrast between "using God" (one of the temptations of Christ, one of the three faces of evil) and "being with and for God" (the first of three components of basic discipleship). Now we can also see a second radical contrast: the proclamation of the kingdom of God (the gracious rule which is characterized by eternal life, hope, peace and love) or acquiescence in another of the great temptations: the kingdoms of the world (social power, political influence) from the hands of Satan (whose very name means divider, accuser and liar, and whose rule leads to death).

In the most basic sense "proclaiming the gospel of the kingdom" means talking to people about Jesus Christ. This is evangelism, telling people the good news. Peter's first letter puts it this way: "You are a chosen people, a royal priesthood, a holy nation, a people belonging to God, that you may declare the praises of him who called you out of darkness into his wonderful light" (1 Pet 2:9). Paul uses similar imagery in calling disciples to work as "Christ's ambassadors" (2 Cor 5:20). It is a great mistake to minimize this simple, personal exercise of sharing the good news with others. The question has well been asked, "If Christianity were suddenly declared illegal, could the authorities find enough evidence among your neighbors, fellow-students or coworkers to convict you of being a Christian?" Proclaiming the gospel is a basic, essential and fundamentally simple task.

It remains true, however, that the task of proclaiming the kingdom of God is much greater than "spiritual obstetrics"—assisting in as many healthy new births as possible. The parables and the Sermon on the Mount make fully clear the claim that God's new order has on the whole of our life: our money, work, sexuality, politics, everything. Ultimately the rule of Christ will extend to the whole of a new heaven and a new earth. Even now it is essential to try to illuminate our present existence, the church, society and culture we live in, with the news of what the rule of God implies. We are given a picture of the "new Jerusalem" of God's kingdom in the Apocalypse; let's declare this reality to our fellow citizens of today's "Babylon." So too, the Bible (not least the Sermon on the Mount and Jesus' teaching in the Gospels) gives us indications of what the rule of God means for economics, politics and other areas of life.[4] The kingdom of God is "righteousness, peace and joy in the Holy Spirit" (Rom 14:17). Part of proclaiming the good news of the kingdom of God is proclaiming the *content* of that righteousness, peace and joy. We will need to beware of translating the gospel into an abstract political, economic or social "package." But with courage, humility and the creativity of the Holy Spirit in communities of committed disciples, *something* can be proclaimed on behalf of God's good rule.

The gospel of the kingdom has implications for the *means*, the *style of expression* we employ, not just the content being conveyed. Jesus and Andrew did not manipulate Simon with their good news. Jesus spoke words of truth, reality and hope. He awed many people because "he taught as one who had authority, and not as their teachers of the law" (Mt 7:29). His authority was the ring of truth and reality he always displayed. Satan is the "father of lies," the accuser and the deceiver (see Jn 8:44; Rev 12:9-10). In short, the proclamation of the kingdom of God has far-reaching implications for all forms and means of communication (including advertising, legal arguments, and so on). The model for all communication by disciples, in any area of life, is precisely the Word of God.[5]

Healing and Exorcism: The Third Task

From the beginning of his public ministry the people were awed not only by Jesus' teaching and preaching but also by his ability to heal the sick and exorcize demons from the possessed. One of Simon's first experiences with Jesus was the healing of his mother-in-law. The disciples were commissioned by Christ to heal the sick and cast out demons. In one of the most stunning miracles Jesus performed, not long after the appointment of the Twelve, the twelve-year-old daughter of Jairus, one of the rulers of the synagogue, was raised to life at

Jesus' command (Mt 9:18-26; Mk 5:21-43; Lk 8:40-56). This was the first of three special episodes where only Peter, James and John accompanied Jesus. All three synoptic Gospels tell us that the crowd laughed at Jesus in disbelief when he said, "Stop wailing . . . She is not dead but asleep." They knew she was dead. But Jesus took her by the hand and said, "My child, get up!" And immediately she got up and walked.

By reason of frequency as well as by explicit declaration of Jesus, healing loomed very large in discipleship as portrayed in the Gospels and Acts. Dozens of healings are described: a deaf-mute, those suffering from hemorrhage, epilepsy, paralysis, blindness, a severed ear (thanks to Peter!) and an eighteen-year-old "spirit of infirmity." The ultimate test, of course, was death. You will recall the raising of Lazarus from the dead, as well as Jairus's daughter—not to mention Jesus' own resurrection.

I believe it is essential to add to this list of maladies three others. First, Jesus worked at healing the psychospiritual problems of anxiety and guilt growing out of people's alienation from God and from themselves. Second, he worked, sometimes miraculously, at healing the devastation of hunger (see Mk 6:30-44; 8:1-10 and parallels). Third, Jesus worked at healing the conflicts between human beings (including those of different race, gender, age, class and so on). In each of these cases there is a profound alienation, a fracturing of human life, which Jesus heals and restores.

At the beginning of his public ministry Jesus announces his "platform" as that of Isaiah 61: "The Spirit of the Lord is on me, because he has anointed me to preach good news to the poor. He has sent me to proclaim freedom for the prisoners and recovery of sight for the blind, to release the oppressed, to proclaim the year of the Lord's favor" (Lk 4:18-19). When John the Baptist in prison asked for evidence that Jesus truly was the Messiah, the message sent back was that the blind, lepers, lame and deaf were healed, the dead were raised and the poor were hearing the good news (Lk 7:22). Healing, in both the specifically medical sense and in the broader context, is essential and central in the ministry of Jesus Christ and in that of his followers.[6]

Healing was often closely associated with exorcism—casting out demons. Referring to the women who had been ill for eighteen years, Jesus said she was bound by Satan in that experience (Lk 13:16) and that her healing amounted to a release from captivity. When the Seventy return from their travels with reports of successful healings, Jesus said that he saw "Satan fall like lightning from heaven" (Lk 10:18). The combat against death, disease and illness of all kinds is nothing less than a combat against the demonic. It is one of the few true species of "holy war."

Healing and exorcism are the third essential activity of discipleship today, as always. Our action (including our vocational existence as well as our volunteer work and other activities) ought to have a healing, restoring, liberating impact on those around us. Satan's attempt to manipulate Jesus' own hunger after forty days of fasting in the wilderness—"Tell these stones to become bread"—met with rebuke. Jesus refused to take orders from Satan; he refused to allow natural necessity to win over spiritual freedom. But in no way did that mean Jesus had no response to hunger or other forms of nature's challenge. Bread and healing would come by the bushel from Jesus and his disciples, but as an act of free compassion and concern. Does Jesus condition his gifts of food or healing on conversion? Never! He does respond to faith—but he responds as well to basic need. Satan's solution to hunger is an attempt to deceive and manipulate; Jesus' actions are gratuitous movements of compassion, freedom and love.

Five brief comments need to be made before concluding this discussion of healing and exorcism. First, the connection between disease or hunger and the demonic is not to be charged to the "victim." Jesus himself made this clear to his disciples who wondered, "Who sinned, this man or his parents . . . ? (Jn 9:2). The answer: neither. We are all caught up in the web of fallen creation and history. It is a mistake to blame people for obviously unavoidable calamities they suffer.

Second, in this ongoing combat not everyone will be healed. Paul, certainly a "Spirit-filled" disciple capable of healing others, could neither be healed himself of his famous "thorn in the flesh" through his many prayers, nor could he heal his friend Trophemus, whom he left "sick in Miletus" (2 Tim 4:20).

Third, the relationship of the demonic principalities and powers to our existence is both mysterious and variable. In some cases today, as well as in the New Testament era, the relationship is spectacular (I'm tempted to say "spooky"!) and perhaps terrifying. In other cases demonic forces work much more subtly and "respectably" but are not for that reason any less malevolent.

Fourth, by the same token, some healing (and some healers) may be charismatic and spectacular.[7] Others will be more mundane, perhaps using ordinary medicine, nutrition, counseling and so on. In our age of the glorified "spectacle" and the "star" we must remember that what counts is faithfulness, not headlines or hokum! Consider teaching as a parallel case: the charismatic orator has no more value intrinsically than the mother or father who faithfully, quietly, haltingly passes on the truth to a child. Both are engaged in proclaming the gospel.

Fifth, none of this is to deny the fact that suffering may be "seized" by God and the sufferer, and may be a means of growth and great value. Peter's first letter has a good deal to say by way of encouraging those who are suffering "innocently"—in this case because of persecution for their faith. However, just as a social order, which persecutes Christians (or others), is "out of joint" with the rule of God so, in a less direct sense perhaps, the physical ecology which lies behind the innocent suffering from cancer, famine and other problems is "out of joint" with the rule of God.

It is important to engage in this kind of effort to understand and explain our fractured world and its pain and suffering. Complete, satisfactory explanation, however, eludes us most of the time. What remains clear is the call to act, to heal and to combat the demonic. Certainly there is broad scope for our action as healers in the world! The fact that Jesus did not heal everyone in the world should free us from being immobilized by the awesome challenge in the world around us. The challenge is to do *something,* not everything. *Someone's* sickness, anxiety, hunger or loneliness ought to be receiving our healing touch. *Some* strife-torn relationship (among our children, a marriage we know, a business-labor dispute and so on) could receive our prayers and our acts of conciliation and peacemaking. *One* world hunger organization, peace-seeking agency or medical research and care facility could use our help.

It is no accident at all that nurses and doctors have often accompanied Christian missionaries into new parts of the world. Often with great personal sacrifice these men and women have sensed the intimate association of healing with the proclamation of the gospel. It is well and good for Christians to go to medical school and throw their energy and ability into the fight against disease and ill health. It "fits" well with the proclamation of the gospel. Unfortunately, some Christian doctors find it nearly impossible to resist the lure of wealth which is available from the hands of weak, frightened, desperate patients. Jesus and the disciples did not get rich on other people's misery. Thus, choosing to be a doctor (or other health care professional) has great promise but does not automatically locate one in faithful relation to Christian discipleship.

But the call to heal applies as much to those in nonmedical vocations as to doctors and nurses and other health care professionals. The question is simple: To what extent am I using my time, energy, abilities and creativity to promote the healing of the earth and its people? Is my business contributing toward death and disease, toward alienation and misery in the world? These are hard questions! There are seldom obvious, clear answers. But if Christians today wish to root their discipleship in that of Peter, the New Testament community and Jesus Christ himself, their lives and activities must manifest a healing dimension. Since Christianity is a "full-time" occupation including the whole of our life every day, then what we do on the job or in school deserves just as much attention as our part-time activities with the church or family.

It might appear that we have been loaded with an awesome, unmanageable burden in this threefold life of discipleship: the life with God, the proclamation of the good news of the kingdom and an active life of healing! It is serious. It is difficult at times. And I do not think a modified job description can be negotiated with our Lord! But if you are weighed down with cares and guilt, you have missed the point. This task is to be undertaken in joy and freedom with your "brother Andrew" and your "buddies James and John." There are parties ahead as well as storms, resurrections as well as insults. The Christian life is a meaning-full adventure in the footsteps of Jesus Christ.

For Reflection or Discussion

1. In your mind, what distinguishes Christian life (discipleship) from non-Christian life—activities, a "style" or "tone," or what? Has your mind changed on this question since you first thought about what is involved in living as a Christian?

2. What have been your most successful ways of "being with God" (think of areas such as your personal life, your family, your church)? What are the major obstacles to this aspect of discipleship for you?

3. What are the best opportunities you can see for carrying out the call to "proclaim the kingdom" and "heal" given the present state of your life (studies, employer, time and so on)? Do either of these two tasks of discipleship pose a threat or difficulty for your job? Do you visualize any exciting new possibilities?

4 Risks & Questions: Discipleship in Motion

*"What is humanly impossible
is possible with God."*

DISCIPLESHIP, THE LIFE OF A FOLLOWER OF JESUS CHRIST, HAS A DEFIN-
able content. There is immense flexibility of specific expression in
different times and places, but all disciples are called to cultivate their
living relationship with Jesus Christ, to speak in ways that proclaim
the good news of God's rule and to act in ways that are healing and
liberating for others. But, there is also a characteristic "style" and
"tone" in the movement of discipleship, that is, in the expression of
the three components of the Christian life. I believe this is best described as the "risk of faith." Discipleship is characterized by a certain,
recurring element of risk, of daring to be and do what is by ordinary
human reckoning impossible. One of the most important expressions
of this risk of faith is "the question"—our question for God *and* his
question for us. Just as Peter's story helps us understand the threefold
content of discipleship, it is his experience that requires us to examine
the "risk" and the "question" as essential requirements for Christian
faithfulness, growth and maturity.[1]

To be sure, there is a certain glorification of "risk takers" in our contemporary culture. Daredevils and professional stunt men like Evel Knievel grow rich off an American appetite for danger and risk. Television shows, movies, circuses and other spectacles staging this type of thing are endless. Many popular spectator sports feature a kind of risk, danger and courting of catastrophe. In fact, however, the popularity of such vicarious thrills is in direct proportion to the banality and boredom of a *security*-seeking culture! What people really want is security, not risk. Thus, endless demands are made on the state to provide various forms of social security. Insurance policies multiply for all conceivable contingencies. With the popularity of guard dogs, weapons, alarm systems, self-defense courses and other forms of protection, it is undeniable that security is the major theme; risk is carefully contained on the screen, stage or field where we can safely watch it. An equally important evidence of this quest for security is the rampant *conformism* of behavior, dress, speech, values and so forth in our culture. Realism, conservatism, conformism—the security of the eighties!

This is not to deny that a minority of our contemporaries do dare to be different and to take a certain kind of risk. Hang gliders and mountain climbers (and pedestrians crossing streets in Paris or San Francisco) risk life and limb even without a paying audience bribing them to do so. Boy George dressed weird even before people paid him to do it. Even so, this minority of practitioners of the reckless, foolhardy and outrageous are often acting out of a kind of nihilism, a kind of "What have I got to lose?" resignation. This is *not* what is meant by "the risk of faith"!

It is tragic that the Christian church is so prone to security and conformism. In any given congregation we tend to look a lot alike, talk alike, live alike. Even worse, the church often represents very faithfully the values and lifestyle of the culture and society in which it lives. This is tragic because nothing is clearer in the Bible than that God is *holy*, that is, "set apart." "Different." In Jesus' choice phrases, he is *in* the world (really, concretely present in the heart of the world and history) but *not of* the world (different in key respects—Jn 17). The people of God, in turn, are to exemplify this "in-but-not-of" life of

God's Spirit. Peter's first letter is addressed "to God's elect, strangers in the world" (1 Pet 1:1). "Live your lives as strangers here" (1:17), he says. Christian disciples are called to live *here*, in *this* world—but as *strangers*, not conformists. There is nothing very "strange" about most of our Christian behavior today! Maybe we need to rediscover the meaning of the "risk of faith."

Peter symbolizes the "risk of faith" that is part of all authentic discipleship in the famous story of his walking on the water, to which we are about to turn. From the very beginning of his relationship with Peter, Jesus was simultaneously an ordinary Jewish carpenter/teacher who dropped in on his home and business, and a man with an extraordinary difference. Jesus was simultaneously the true Son of man and the true Son of God. The miraculous catch of fish, the healing of Peter's mother-in-law, the raising of Jairus's daughter and the feeding of the five thousand hungry people—these were stunning exceptions to "business as usual." No less stunning, however, was his strangely personal news for Simon: "You will be the Rock!"

For the crowds as well as the disciples, Jesus' manner and message were radically different from the norm: "Never a man spoke like this!" Jesus startled his disciples when he "spoke with a woman" (a Samaritan, no less) about worship and righteousness (Jn 4). He surprised them by warmly welcoming children (Mk 10:13-16 and parallels). Perhaps most incredible of all was his response to his own unjust treatment. Peter described it in his letter many years later: " 'He committed no sin, and no deceit was found in his mouth.' When they hurled their insults at him, he did not retaliate; when he suffered, he made no threats. Instead, he entrusted himself to him who judges justly" (1 Pet 2:22-23). In this, Peter says, he was "leaving you an example, that you should follow in his steps" (1 Pet 2:21).

Walking on water was not Peter's first risk of faith either. He risked being a public fool, and having to put all his fishing equipment away again, when he let out his nets at Jesus' command. He risked his business and family when he left all to follow Jesus. When he and the others started walking around the crowd of five thousand to hand out only five loaves and two fish, he might have wondered what would happen if the small food supply ran out before this hungry mob received what was promised! Risk is not a rare and exceptional feature of the Christian life, it is a recurring dimension in the movement of faithful discipleship.

Risk means the refusal to be shaped by the world as it is. It is a refusal to be cowed by tradition, realism, "the facts" or social pressure. It is an act of freedom and a breaking of bondage. It is an insistence on reopening situations that appear closed, on following a third alternative when only two seem to be available. "Lazarus has been dead for four days!" "There are only five loaves and two fish to feed this huge crowd!" "We have already fished here all night and caught nothing!" "The Law of Moses says this woman caught in adultery must be stoned!" "The Jews have no dealings with the Samaritans!" "Marriage without divorce is nearly impossible!" "It's easier for a camel to go through the eye of a needle than for a rich man to enter the kingdom of God!" "People sink when they try to walk on water!"

To all of this, Jesus and his fellow "riskers" reply: "SO WHAT! What is humanly impossible, is possible with God!" (Lk 18:27, on the difficulty of the rich being saved!). *Maybe* the situation is closed. But *maybe not!* If God himself can enter human history in Jesus Christ, if God can carry out the Great Miracle, the resurrection from the dead, then anything is possible.

The Walk on the Water (Mt 14:22-23; Mk 6:45-52; Jn 6:16-21)[2]

Peter and the disciples had just spent a lot of time and energy in helping Jesus feed five thousand hungry people. They needed to get home across the Sea of Galilee to Bethsaida and Capernaum, and it was going to get dark soon. Jesus convinced the disciples to leave without him while he stayed behind to dismiss the crowd (which now wanted to pressure him to become their king!) and then to have time alone for prayer.

Perhaps the disciples were a little slow in shoving off from land in their boat. In any event, as Jesus ended his prayers alone on the land, he could see that a mile or so from the shore (Mt 14:24, many "furlongs," that is, many "eighths of a mile") they were having great difficulty making progress against a stiff wind. Still, it was not until the fourth watch of the night (the last one before dawn) that Jesus decided to walk across the sea. By this time it was too dark and they were too far ("three or three and a half miles" Jn 6:19) to be seen from land any longer.

Why did Jesus walk across the water? Because he wanted to "come to them," to his disciples. But then (a little strangely!) "he was about to pass them" (Mk 6:48). Too late! The disciples in the boat had spotted a figure walking on the sea and were terrified, thinking it was a ghost. Jesus then decided not to pass by them and called out "It is I. Don't be afraid."

At this, Peter's panic turned immediately to excitement and anticipation. What a chance! Our Lord can walk on water without sinking. So he called out, "Lord, if it's you . . . tell me to come to you on the water." Jesus replied, "Come." Matthew continues the story:

> Then Peter got down out of the boat, walked on the water and
> came toward Jesus. But when he saw the wind, he was afraid and,
> beginning to sink, cried out, "Lord, save me!" Immediately Jesus
> reached out his hand and caught him. "You of little faith," he said,
> "why did you doubt?" (Mt 14:29-31)

So they both got into the boat, the wind died down and they made it to their destination. Matthew says those in the boat "worshipped" Jesus and said, "Truly you are the Son of God." According to Mark, they were astounded by the Lord's walk on the water but still had not understood what happened even with the loaves of bread and the multitude because their "hearts were hardened."

To begin with, the most amazing part of this story (the one part reported by three of the Gospels: Matthew, Mark and John) is not Peter's short stroll on the water, but that of Jesus. As in other of Jesus' miracles, he acted in a way that radically contradicted the laws of nature and ordinary human experience. As we will see, however, he did this (here as always) in compliance with the law of God, that is, with the will and purpose of God. Jesus' miracles were *never* capricious displays of magic to entertain the crowds *or* to save himself from ordinary human toil and trial. This is why he often asked those who had been healed not to talk about it to others. His interest was in helping the victim, not in gaining a reputation as a great miracle worker.

How did Jesus succeed in his own risk of walking across the Sea of Galilee (or in his other miracles)? How did he manage to do the incredible? "Who is this? He commands even the winds and the water, and they obey him" (Lk 8:25). "How did this man get such learning without having studied?" (Jn 7:15). In many different discussions and descriptions in the New Testament we are assured that Jesus was "like his brothers in every way" (Heb 2:17), that he was "tempted in every way, just as we are" (Heb 4:15), that he really was "made in human likeness" (Phil 2:7), and that he really was made of regular human "flesh" (Jn 1:14).

What allowed Jesus to transcend the limitations of nature and reason was the power of the transcendent, infinite God with whom he was united. He lived as perfect "man for God," in perfect, unbroken communion with God the Father, with unshakable determination to do the will of God. As Jesus put it, "By myself I can do nothing" (Jn 5:30). "The words I say to you are not just my own. Rather, it is the Father, living in me, who is doing his work" (Jn 14:10). The words and the works of Jesus are the words and works of the "Wholly Other" God, present in a real human being, allowing him to go beyond ordinary, finite human possibilities. Jesus, however, is the only example of perfect, absolute faith, on the one hand, and perfect, absolute freedom from sin, on the other. In him the power of God was not impeded by sin and the resistance of an imperfect nature such as we have. The power of God was unrestricted in Jesus Christ. The "how" of Jesus' miraculous life is explained by the power of God. "The Father is greater than I" but "I and the Father are one" (Jn 14:28; 10:30).

The "how" of Peter's (and any other disciple's) miraculous possibilities is also the presence of faith. Faith, as discussed in chapter one, is what binds us to Jesus Christ, to God. It is not just a "believing that" certain things are true about God. It is a "believing *on*," a trusting, a grasping and seizing of Jesus Christ. It is an opening up of our life and a determination to let God take charge and work in us. Sin is just the opposite. Sin is a closing off from God and a reliance on the self as we face life. We human beings were made by and for God; sin is the choice not to live by and for God. Peter walked on the water so long as he was linked by rash faith to the power of God in Jesus Christ.

He began to sink when the winds and waves distracted him from this God-connection, and self-regard, circumstance-regard took over. However little his faith was, however briefly or imperfectly it was demonstrated, Peter *did* walk on the water! As Jesus said, his followers would be able to do the same great works he did (and even greater!) by dependence on the power of God: Father, Son and Holy Spirit (see Jn 14:12-13).

Equally important with the *how* are the *why* and the *when* of the risk of faith. The *when* is not "any time." The *why* is not "any reason." It is no accident that Jesus' walk on the water happens *when* he has prayed. God supplies the why and the when, as well as the power to take the risk. It is an exact parallel that Peter walks on the water only *when* his Lord has called him to come. Any study of the life of Jesus in the Gospels will show his extraordinary prayer life.[3] The risk of faith can only succeed when God's guidance is being followed. It cannot be followed or detected if it is not sought!

A careful look at the various accounts of this episode in the Gospels shows that the reasons for this risk of faith, the "why," are to be discovered in the threefold "program" of Jesus described in the previous chapter on the content of discipleship. It is, I repeat, neither gratuitous magic for the crowds nor avoidance of the longer walk home on land. Jesus walked across the sea to "come to them," to be with and perhaps even to preserve his community. Jesus' walk manifested his desire to have these followers "with him" as well as his readiness to save them and overcome the threat of death, should their boat be in serious trouble.

As it turned out, they *were* successfully making it across the sea, though slowly and with difficulty. Therefore "he was about to pass by them" undetected. Since the disciples discovered him, he came to join them. A second purpose then emerges in what follows with Peter. Peter's faith in him, his reckless openness to attempting the impossible, becomes an opportunity to teach the disciples more about the power of the "rule of God." The "why" of Peter's walking on water is clear from the context. It is to teach the "risk of faith."

What, then, can we learn from Peter's walk on the water? First, it is important to be open to the impossible—to be willing to get up out of our little boat and do what is by natural inclination, worldly realism, social custom and even "common sense" impossible. It is to believe that "what is impossible with men is possible with God" (Lk 18:27). No less than walking on water, loving and forgiving an enemy, suffering unjustly, giving away hard-earned money, standing alone for righteousness and justice, changing jobs, moving residences, giving scarce time to prayer and worship, reconciling with your spouse— many things will strike us as totally impossible. But with God they become possible. We must be not only open but as eager as Peter to find out whether this is so.

Second, what Peter is going to attempt is what has already been done by Jesus Christ. It is no greater than what our Lord has already done. It is no different. Christian risk is never nihilistic, chaotic or undirected. It is precise and meaningful. We may take heart that not only has Jesus gone ahead of us in our risk, many other faithful brothers and sisters have done so as well. We have their examples to learn from; we have their successes to inspire us.

Third, when Peter falters the Lord is there to extend a hand and rescue him. It is not only at the beginning but throughout the risk of faith that Jesus is with us. He is not a Lord who gives orders and then watches. He is the Lord who is always with us, ready to help us even when faith and certainty are not perfect.

Fourth, it is Peter who takes the risk for himself. He does not put his fellow disciples in jeopardy. There is risk to himself (if that *was* a ghost out there and not really the Lord!). His friends and family might lose him, and that is an important consideration. But the risk is primarily for himself. He bears the primary burden of the consequences of his choice. He is not going to capsize the boat if he sinks. If our own risk is going to involve the substantial interest of others around us (family, business, and so on), we must accept this reality and proceed with a degree of patience and love. If a group is going to share the consequences of a risk, they should share the conviction that it is in fact a call by God to do so.

Finally, Peter checks to make sure it really is the Lord who is calling to him. He waits to hear his voice clearly say "Come." Getting out of the boat without clearly seeing and hearing the call of the Lord would be folly and suicide, not the risk of faith. The disciples in the boat also saw and heard the Lord call Peter. They could confirm to him that it was not a ghost or his imagination. Jesus sent his disciples out "two-by-two" not "one-by-one." Discernment of the voice of God is a joint effort as well as an individual task. Lacking a visible, physical Jesus before our eyes, it is all the more important for a disciple to pray for guidance and hear the Word of God in community with others. Rarely are Christians called to act as Lone Rangers. Those around us may be wrong. It may be that God calls us to go against all advice. But the burden of proof is on the person who takes a risk when his or her call is totally unrecognized by other committed disciples actively praying and seeking the Word of God with that individual. The normal pattern for discipleship, now that Jesus is resurrected and ascended from this earth, is for the "voice of Christ" to be heard in the Word of God and in the body of Christ (our fellow Christians). So too, the rescuing or helping hand of Christ today will normally be extended through our Christian brothers or sisters.

"Getting out of the boat" for the risk of faith may be as mundane in practice as telephoning someone with whom you wish to be reconciled.[4] Or it may be as threatening as quitting a secure but ethically suspect job. It is essential that we be prepared and open to do such things. They are part of the ongoing style and tone of discipleship. Since our Lord promises to be with us at all times, we can approach the risk of faith with joy, confidence and eager anticipation, not with the anxiety and fear of those without faith. With God *all* things are possible.

Bringing Our Questions to God

Walking on water was the most spectacular "risk of faith" taken by Simon Peter. Another aspect of the movement of discipleship, another kind of "risk," is that of bringing questions to Jesus Christ.[5] The Gospels are filled with questions, and Peter contributes more than his share! In posing a question, one is asking for a response. In posing a question to Jesus Christ, one is inviting not "neutral information" but the Word of God. This Word is truth, cutting through all deception, evasion and ignorance. It is life because it expresses the reality of God. It is always a kind of risk to ask God for an answer because the Word of God is a response that transcends the question. It goes beyond, and often against, our expectations. God's answer brings growth and maturity if it is heard; it brings judgment if it is rejected. For to reject the Word of God is to reject life.

A legitimate question is not always recognizable by punctuation, by the presence or absence of the question mark at the end. A question may be implied by a hesitant assertion which invites comment. A question may be posed by a fearful or even a blank look on the face! On the other hand, a phrase with a question mark on the end may be a rhetorical device, a disguised affirmation. We must recall that the first tactic of the serpent with Adam and Eve was to put God in question: "Did God really say . . . ?" (Gen 3:1). The serpent was "subtle" in this regard. The question leads directly to an overt contradiction of the Word of God: "You will not surely die" (Gen 3:4). So, too, the opponents of Jesus often formulated questions "to trap him," "to entangle him in his talk" and "to test him." For example, in Matthew 22 (Mk 12; Lk 20) the Pharisees and Herodians ask him about politics and taxes, then the Sadducees come at him with a tricky question about marriage and the resurrection (they didn't even believe in resurrection!), and finally a lawyer (then, as now, the master of the trick question!) asked about the greatest commandment of the Law. Jesus' responses are overwhelming and, as the phony questioners slink away, the crowds are astonished.

Still, Jesus clearly said, "Ask and it will be given to you; seek and you will find" (Mt 7:7; Lk 11:9). This invitation includes permission to ask God for information, for answers to our questions. Thus Nicodemus asked, "How can a man be born when he is old?" (Jn 3:4). The Samaritan woman asked, "How can you [a Jew] ask me [a Samaritan woman] for a drink?" (Jn 4:9). The disciples asked, "What must we do to do the works God requires?" (Jn 6:28). In these and many other cases the question is rewarded by Jesus with awesome words of love, truth and guidance.

Peter's questions are sometimes misguided: "What about him?" he asked, nosing into Jesus' plans for another disciple (Jn 21:21)! "Lord, are you going to wash my feet?" he asks, resisting Jesus' move (Jn

13:6). Sometimes they are self-regarding: "We have left everything to follow you! What then will there be for us?" (Mt 19:27). "Is it I who will betray you?" (Mk 14:19). Sometimes they are simple but well-directed requests by a man who wants to be with Christ: "Where do you want us to prepare [the Passover]?" (Lk 22:9). "Where are you going?" "Can't I follow you?" (Jn 13:36-38).

Peter is the one who asks for more explanation about a parable's meaning (Mt 15:15), about the curious withering of a fig tree (Mt 21:20; Mk 11:21), about when the future kingdom of God will come (Mk 13:3-4), and about whether Jesus' teaching is for the disciples or applies to everyone (Lk 12:41). In a moment of high drama he asks if he should strike with the sword against those who have come to arrest Jesus (Lk 22:49-50; Jn 18:10-11) but makes the mistake of acting before the answer from Jesus (an emphatic "Put your sword back in its place . . . for all who draw the sword will die by the sword—Mt 26:52). Finally, Peter's provocative question, "How many times shall I forgive my brother when he sins against me? Up to seven times?" brings Jesus' reply "Seventy-seven times" (Mt 18:21-22) and the magnificent parable of the unforgiving servant.

Thus Peter carried on his relationship with Jesus partly by asking him questions. In return he was guided, corrected, illuminated, stretched and matured. Even his "dumbest" and simplest questions resulted positively for his growth because they were directed to the Word of God. Jesus did not refuse to answer Peter. In fact, as we have seen, he invited such questioning.

In our own era this questioning process is essential for Christian growth and maturity. It is not only appropriate but *urgent* for contemporary disciples to bring their questions to the Word of God. We have already been doing this here by coming to the New Testament asking, "What really is conversion?" and "What is the true meaning of discipleship?" We ought also to ask what Jesus has to say about money, about marriage, about justice and politics. Aside from what university textbooks say about business administration, what does the Bible have to say? What does Jesus have to say about being single? About the afterlife? About truth in advertising? What does he have to say about care for the earth and its resources? About the philosophy and interpretation of history? About social change?

Jesus is not just Lord of the interior life and the afterlife! Nor is he concerned only with personal life, family life and church life! All of these things are important. But Jesus is the Word of God to the whole of life, including our education, work and leisure in a traffic-congested, computer-infested, violent, urbanized, noisy, anonymous twentieth-century society. Of course there is a risk involved in bringing the questions of your life to the Word of God! You may well, like Peter, get an answer you do not expect or want. It may go against your natural inclination and your security. It may be complex and difficult, requiring a long, patient process of reflection on its implications. But if we wish to live in the footsteps of Jesus Christ, we must risk such questions! A halfway Christian life is not just a betrayal of the claim Christ wishes to place on your life. It is an abandonment of the adventure of being one of God's joyful strangers in the heart of the world.

Hearing God's Questions to Us

There is another side to this questioning process which often is left out of the discussion. This is the reverse of the preceding, that is, quietly and courageously listening to God's questions for us. In the experience of Simon Peter, God's questions in Jesus Christ were finally much more important and decisive than the ones Peter posed to Jesus! Just as God's responding to our questions is a process extending from beginning to end in the Bible, so too God is continually putting questions to men and women throughout Scripture. Thus, in the Genesis story of Adam and Eve's sin, God comes asking, "Where are you?" and "What have you done?" (Gen 3:9-13). To Cain, the murderer of Abel, God asks, "Where is your brother?" (Gen 4:9). Job's multiple questions have occupied commentators for centuries; but more decisive are the questions God puts to Job!

Thus, Jesus asks Peter (after the walk on the water), "Why did you doubt?" (Mt 14:31). "What do you think, Simon?" (about the temple tax issue, Mt 17:25). To all of his disciples Jesus asked: "Why do you call me, 'Lord, Lord,' and do not do what I say?" (still relevant! Lk 6:46). Again, "When I sent you out [the Twelve on their missions], did you lack anything?" (not a thing, actually! Lk 22:35). And "Who is greater, the one who is at the table or the one who serves? . . . But I am among you as one who serves," Jesus said (Lk 22:27). The big question was this: "Who do you say I am?" (Mt 16:15; Mk 8:29; Lk 9:20). The disciples and crowds made many great statements about who Jesus was while in the flush of a miraculous success. But what did they really think in a sober reflection?

In his own most difficult hours in the garden of Gethsemane, Jesus questioned Peter, James and John: "Are you asleep? Could you not keep watch for one hour?" And a second and third time: "Are you still sleeping and resting?" (Mk 14:37-41 and parallels). In another three-fold question after Peter's denial, the Lord asked, "Simon son of John, do you truly love me more than these?" (Jn 21:15-17). It is very clear that Jesus' questions were even more significant for Peter's discipleship than were Peter's questions for the Lord.

Jesus' questions (and, more generally, the questions which God poses in Scripture) are extremely important because they represent *God's* agenda and not just ours. God is interested in our questions and, indeed, welcomes them. But he has his own questions for us, and it is altogether possible that his agenda includes different priorities than our own. A modern heart specialist, for example, may believe that the most pressing question is that of the ethical ramifications of using animal or mechanical hearts in transplant operations to save lives. A criminal lawyer may be most troubled about the issue of confidentiality when she knows a vicious crime has been covered up. A Christian in Congress may be most concerned about the budget deficit and the morality of interest rates affected by that deficit. But suppose we ask God what his most important ethical concern is today. I suspect he would reply that the number-one issue now, as in the past, is idolatry: the first commandment is, "You shall have no other gods before me."

To be questioned by God today means to read and hear that command as a personal question. Are there any ways in which I might be allowing rival gods to threaten the rightful place of Jesus Christ? What am I worshiping today? That is, what am I sacrificing my time and effort toward? Where is my loyalty being demonstrated? This is only one simple example. The point is that we should study the life and teaching of our Lord and ask honestly, "What changes does this imply for me?" We should read Scripture not just with our list of questions in hand, but with a blank piece of paper on which to note the questions God brings to us from the text. This is also why it is important to read through the whole Bible regularly, and not just the chapters we find especially comforting, easy and reassuring.

But there is a risk! As in Peter's experience, God's questions will cut through our masks and defenses. They may judge us and threaten us in very immediate and personal ways. Unlike some of our "God wants you to feel good about yourself" and "Let's all be warm and comfortable in this church" sermons of today, there will be a "No" heard along with God's "Yes." The way of Jesus Christ is not a comforting illusion. It is life, reality and truth. It is about tough love, uncompromising justice and righteousness. It is also total forgiveness and free grace. If it is worth anything, it is worth everything.

Following Jesus Christ involves you in the greatest risk of your life. You must leave everything. You must lose your life and take up your own cross. But if you have faith—that is, if you seize on to Jesus Christ as your Lord—you will find that a much greater life, the life of the resurrection, is yours. You will never know what it is to walk on the water until you take the risk of getting out of the boat.

There is a choice between two "packages" here. On the one hand there is the ultimately banal, conservative security and conformism of our "advanced" postindustrial civilization, which allows you the privilege of being a spectator at an unending circus of vicarious thrills and risks of no real threat to your comfort. On the other hand, there is the genuinely gripping, challenging adventure of the risk of faith in Jesus Christ. This, in turn, is related to a deep, unshakable security in the eternal God. As Peter, the water-walker, put it at the end of his life of faith, we are "shielded by God's power," "born of imperishable seed," "chosen and preserved" by God, able at all times to "entrust our souls to a faithful Creator," knowing that our future, our inheritance "can never perish, spoil, or fade" (1 Pet). The risk of faith is not without its own context of security, but this is in stark contrast to the security fashioned out of bulging bank accounts or muscles, social acceptance or state paternalism!

For Reflection or Discussion

1. What "risks" have you taken in your life? Would you call them "risks of faith"? What made you decide to take them? Did you begin to "sink" at any point? How did the experiences turn out?

2. What are the most crucial questions you would like God to answer in your personal life? in your school or professional life?

3. What do you think might be three or four questions God would like to ask of the contemporary Christian individual or church?

Do you love me because
  you need me?

Or do you need me because
  you love me?

5 Building on the Rock: The Meaning of the Church

"You are the Christ, the Son of the Living God!"

CHURCH IS OFTEN EITHER THE BEST PART OF A CHRISTIAN'S EXPERIENCE today or the worst! At its best, gathering in the church is like an oasis in a desert. Nothing can compare with the love, acceptance and fellowship of caring brothers and sisters. Few experiences are as great as the presence of Christ among us as we sing, pray and worship at the Lord's Table. No university lecture or political speech can convey the truth, reality and life of a good sermon exhibiting the Word of God in the power of the Spirit.

But, alas, nothing is as disappointing as the aggravating dullness of an unprepared, uninspired speech by a pastor who is uninflamed by the Word of God (if it were a college course, we would drop it from our study list immediately). Few experiences are more torturous than having to submit to a diet of heartless, thoughtless, disharmonic, insipid congregational music (if we were home, we would sprint to the stereo to change the dial). No personal affront hurts as deeply as the snub or neglect from a clique in our home church (only a desperate sense of obligation makes us return). A significant number of Christians are disciples of Jesus Christ *in spite of* their experience of the church!

Nothing is as simple as leaving church B and moving to church A, as though that would solve the problem. Most churches (like most members of churches) are like Peter: when they are good, they're wonderful; when they are bad, they're terrible! Most churches have strengths as well as weaknesses. In an odd sort of way, a mature disciple can find encouragement even in the weakest, most banal performance of his or her church, for this bears unimpeachable witness to the grace and humor of God in accepting us talentless, mediocre beggars into his community! Beware of the "perfect church" anyway; its perfection may arise from its insulation from the poverty and suffering around it. The cutting edge of the justice, truth and sacrificial love of the Word of God may have been toned down and softened. The wonderful music and interpersonal communication skills may reflect a bogus imitation of the world rather than the authenticity of Jesus.

But these are generalized observations and the question is what to make of our particular, concrete church experience. You are probably in (or on the edge of) a local church. How can you strengthen what is good and reform what is unacceptably defective? What model or standard can you employ? Should you enroll in a church renewal course at the glittering Crystal Cathedral to find out how Robert Schuller and his team run their church? Should you intern at Sojourners' Fellowship or the radical/biblical Church of the Savior in downtown Washington, D.C.? The possibilities for visiting and learning from other church models are almost endless. The variety is astonishing: from a Presbyterian church oriented to strong, biblical preaching, to a Pentecostal congregation swaying with ecstatic, heartfelt praise to Jesus; from the intricate liturgical forms and symbols, robes, incense and bells in an Episcopal cathedral, to a simple weekly celebration of the Lord's Supper by a small Plymouth Brethren meeting which refuses all notions of clergy, written order of worship or other trappings of "Christendom."

Ralph Martin's book *The Family and the Fellowship* suggests that there are at least four prominent models of the church on the contemporary scene.[1] First, the church is sometimes viewed as a *classroom* or lecture hall with its primary function being learning and instruction. Second, it is sometimes seen as a *theater* in which one comes to view a performance. Third, the church is sometimes treated as a kind of *business corporation*, packaging and marketing religion as efficiently as possible. Or fourth, it might be viewed as a *social club* meeting people's needs for personal relationships and good feelings.

None of these "ideal types" is adequate as a model for the reform of the church. There is a kernel of truth in each type, of course: the church is to be a place of learning, of witness to the dramas reenacting the central events of the faith, of aggressive outreach and propagation of the gospel, and of warm fellowship. In the end, however, neither reflection on "ideal types" or field trips to existing churches will be enough. For reform of the church we must go back to the roots in a determined effort to discover what Jesus had in mind when he founded the church.

For New Testament direction on the structure and activities of the church, recourse is made most often to the great Pauline texts, especially the letter to the Ephesians. It is also Paul's letters to Timothy and Titus which contain the lists of qualifications for elders (bishops, presbyters) and deacons, usually quoted in church constitutions. The descriptions of the early church in Acts are sometimes given attention by church renewal leaders. All of this is essential. What happens, though, if we turn to Peter for illumination on the subject of the church? This is a promising possibility that is rarely pursued.

The term "church" *(ecclesia)*, while frequently appearing in Acts and the letters of the New Testament, only appears three times in the Gospel accounts of our Lord: once in Matthew 16:18 and twice in Matthew 18:17.[2] Peter precipitates the first mention with his great confession of Jesus as the Christ at Caesarea Philippi. He is also present with Jesus and the disciples at the second episode. Furthermore, Peter gives the "inaugural sermon" for the church on Pentecost, he is one of its first great leaders, and he writes about the church in his letters in extremely helpful ways. What can we learn from Peter about the church? How did it all begin?

On This Rock I Will Build My Church (Mt 16:13-23; Mk 8:27-33; Lk 9:18-22)

Peter and the other disciples now had months of experience following Jesus of Nazareth. They had had quiet times of discussion with him, and they had been with him in tumultuous crowds. They had heard astonishing words of wisdom in the Sermon on the Mount and in tense questioning by intellectuals as well as common laborers. They had seen spectacular miracles contradicting nature as well as an equally spectacular love for people of every imaginable type. They had been separated from Jesus for periods of time when they went out on missions two-by-two. They discovered that his "way" was true even out of his immediate presence.

Coming to the villages of Caesarea Philippi, about thirty miles north of Bethsaida and Capernaum, Jesus and the disciples were finally alone together for some prayer and discussion. After his prayers, Jesus turned to his disciples with the question: "Who do people say the Son of Man is?" "Some say John the Baptist; others say Elijah; and still others, Jeremiah or one of the prophets," they responded. "Who do you say I am?" Jesus continued. Simon Peter replied: "You are the Christ, the Son of the living God."

Jesus' response to Peter's famous "confession at Caesarea Philippi" needs to be quoted in full:

> Blessed are you, Simon son of Jonah, for this was not revealed to you by man, but by my Father in heaven. And I tell you that you are Peter [the Rock], and on this rock I will build my church, and the gates of Hades will not overcome it. I will give you the keys of the kingdom of heaven; whatever you bind on earth will be bound in heaven, and whatever you loose on earth will be loosed in heaven.

Then Jesus told the disciples not to publicize this yet. It was not yet the appropriate time.

Unfortunately, Peter did not have much time to savor this great compliment or to explore in detail the extraordinary promise Jesus had just given him! For Jesus then continued his teaching by clarifying to them that he must go to Jerusalem, suffer many things and be rejected by the elders, chief priests and scribes, culminating in his being put to death. Perhaps Peter didn't hear the last line of what Jesus said: "And on the third day [I will] be raised to life." At any rate, Peter blurted out "Never, Lord! . . . This shall never happen to you!" Jesus turned to Peter and said, "Get behind me, Satan! You are a stumbling block to me; you do not have in mind the things of God, but the things of men." Peter kept his mouth shut this time.

Jesus concluded by saying to his disciples, "If anyone would come after me, he must deny himself and take up his cross and follow me. For whoever wants to save his life will lose it, but whoever loses his life for me will find it. What good will it be for a man if he gains the whole world, yet forfeits his soul? Or what can a man give in exchange for his soul?" The "Son of Man," Jesus said (referring to himself) is going to come in the glory of the Father very soon! At that point, repayment for losing one's life will be made by God.

Peter's experience at Caesarea Philippi reminds us first of all how common it is for human weaknesses to be closely related to one's strengths. The psychologist or therapist is sometimes deeply troubled and suicidal. The intellectually brilliant sometimes display astonishing stupidity. The forceful apologist may wrestle with deep personal doubt. The paradigm of generosity sometimes conceals a streak of pettiness and selfishness. The ethicist who inspires an iron determination to discover and do the good may be weak as water in other ways and capable of torturous rationalizations about personal disobedience. These are only samples and general observations.

Negatively, the lesson for all of us is very clear: "Let him who stands, take heed lest he fall" (1 Cor 10:12 KJV). Positively, what seems to be happening in the Christian life is that God's "power is made perfect in weakness" (2 Cor 12:9). That is, the best counselor may very well be a person who knows what it is to struggle psychologically. The most powerful apologist may be someone who knows best the grip of doubt. The best ethical guidance may be given by someone who has struggled intensely with evil. This is not a "necessary" relationship, but it is frequently observable and worth our reflection. Realism and humility are the negative, cautionary lesson; hope and trust in God are the positive side to all this.

So it happens that the greatest apostle of love (John of Zebedee) was created out of a "son of thunder" who suggested the obliteration of some inhospitable Samaritan villagers. And the solid rock (Peter), the bold confessor of Jesus Christ, was at the same time capable of being the unstable voice of Satan himself. This, note well, is day one in the New Testament teaching about the meaning of the church!

Everything begins when the question of Jesus Christ is heard by the disciples. Everything turns on who Jesus is. *Everything*. If he is God, then everything becomes possible for the disciples. If he is just another great prophet, then they are no more than devotees of another guru in the world. Actually, both the disciples and the crowds had already made many great statements about who Jesus really was. After a day with Jesus, with the excitement of the crowds and John the Baptist's identification of Jesus as the "Lamb of God," Andrew told his brother "We have found the Messiah" (Jn 1:41). After the miracle of the great catch of fish on his "conversion" day, Peter called Jesus "Lord" (Lk 5:8). After Jesus' walk on the water, the disciples said with astonishment, "Truly you are the Son of God" (Mt 14:33).

But it is one thing to make noble statements in the flush of success or a great miracle or first love. It is another to answer Jesus' question in the stillness and quiet after really getting to know him. It is also one thing to participate in a general public opinion—"The people think you are a great prophet!"—and another to answer for oneself to Jesus Christ, "You are the Christ, the Son of the living God!" The church was not to be founded and built on public opinion. Even today it is a betrayal of Jesus Christ to create a "republican Jesus" or "capitalist Jesus" or an "I'm okay, you're okay Jesus" in order to play to the climate of opinion. The church may be flooded with new members as a result of these tactics, but then it is our own religious club and not the church of Jesus Christ that is being built. The same thing must be said about a "Marxist Jesus," "hippie Jesus," "Aryan Jesus" or any other kind except the biblical Jesus. This leads us to conclude six things.

First, the church is the community of those who confess that Jesus is the Christ, the Son of the Living God.

Second, it is a community blessed by God because it has heard the revelation of God himself. Its confession is not based on "flesh and blood," on human reason or experience, but on the Word of God the Father heard and accepted in Jesus Christ.

Third, this community of confession and revelation, the church, will be built "on the Rock." There have been three popular interpretations of this promise. According to John Calvin (and many other Protestants), the "rock" was not Peter himself but his confession of faith in Jesus as Christ and Son of the Living God. According to Martin Luther, Augustine and others, the "rock" on which the church is to be built is Jesus himself. In this interpretation we must imagine that Jesus pointed first at Simon and said "You are the Rock," and then, pointing back at himself, said, "On *this* Rock I will build my church." Finally, according to the Catholic tradition, and also Protestants such as Zwingli, Cullmann and others, Jesus meant Peter himself is the rock. This is the simplest and most obvious way to read the story, of course.

Our interpretation of this phrase is assisted a great deal by later comments by both Peter and Paul. First, there is Peter's discussion in his first letter:

As you come to him [Jesus Christ], the living Stone—rejected by men but chosen by God and precious to him—you also, like living stones, are being built into a spiritual house to be a holy priesthood, offering spiritual sacrifices acceptable to God through Jesus Christ. For in Scripture it says:

"See, I lay a stone in Zion,
a chosen and precious cornerstone,
and the one who trusts in him
will never be put to shame."

Now to you who believe, this stone is precious. But to those who do not believe,

"The stone the builders rejected
has become the capstone,"

and,

"A stone that causes men to stumble
and a rock that makes them fall."

They stumble because they disobey the message—which is also what they were destined for. (1 Pet 2:4-8)

In the imagery of this text, Jesus is the cornerstone and *the* living stone. But Christians are also constituted as living stones in the construction of this building by "trusting in him," by believing and obeying the Word.

Paul's comments add further clarity to this picture:

[Christians are] built on the foundation of the apostles and prophets, with Christ Jesus himself as the chief cornerstone. In him the whole building is joined together and rises to become a holy temple in the Lord. And in him you too are being built together to become a dwelling in which God lives by his Spirit. (Eph 2:20-22)

Since each of these texts discusses the church in terms of a building made of rocks or stones (and I fail to see a difference between those two terms), we may summarize as follows. The church is like a building, a temple in which God's Spirit lives, a temple which is alive with praise to God in his presence. Though all disciples are "living stones" like their Lord, and like Peter and the original apostles, there remains an important difference. The apostles and prophets alone are the foundation of this building. Peter is "the Rock" on whom the church is built in that he was the spokesman for the apostles. As revealed to him by God the Father, he articulated the word of confession and faith in Jesus Christ. Without Jesus Christ, Peter is nothing and the foundation and building are nothing. Thus, Jesus is the cornerstone, holding everything together.

Fourth, Jesus promises in Matthew: "I will build my church." As it turns out, Jesus will work through his followers. He wants the complicity and assistance of his people. But *Jesus* will build it. It will grow by his strength and in the way and timing he chooses. Furthermore, it must always be remembered that it is "my church," it belongs to *Jesus* not to us. The church does not belong to Peter or his successors, whether those are understood to be the Catholic popes or Christians in general. For this reason it is very important to be careful about what we do in and to the church (locally, denominationally or on any level). It belongs to someone else: Jesus. We must note also that Jesus *will build* his church. Not even the "gates of Hades" or the "powers of death" can prevail against it. In spite of all opposition and all failure by those in and out of the church, Jesus has been building his church, and nothing will stop him from finishing it!

Fifth, to Peter and his successors in the church are committed "the keys of the kingdom of heaven." This is the task and the privilege of opening for other people the gateway to eternal life. In the immediate context, the contrast is to the "gates of Hades," the grave and death. Not long after this in Matthew's Gospel, Jesus also declared: "Woe to you, teachers of the law and Pharisees, you hypocrites! You shut the kingdom of heaven in [people's] faces. You yourselves do not enter, nor will you let those enter who are trying to" (Mt 23:13-14). The church then is the community that can open the gates of heaven and life to people. It is commissioned to "declare the praises of him who called [us] out of darkness into his wonderful light" (1 Pet 2:9). A legitimate church will be a witnessing, evangelizing church which has and uses the keys to the kingdom, which prepares its members to go out two-by-two with the good news of the kingdom of God.

Sixth, the church is to be a community of ethical discipline and freedom. "Whatever you bind on earth will be bound in heaven, and whatever you loose on earth will be loosed in heaven."[3] That this responsibility was not just given to Peter is clear from Jesus' statements in Matthew 18 and John 20 (to *all* the disciples). The text of Matthew 18:15-22 has to do with cases of "a brother sinning against you" and procedures for discipline and forgiveness. (This is also the context where the word *church* is used for only the second and third times in the Gospels.) In both Matthew 16 and Matthew 18 this "binding and loosing" (a common way of referring to moral decision making among the Jewish rabbis at the time) refers to "prohibiting" and "permitting," "allowing" and "disallowing" certain behavior. Despite the failure of the disciples at the time of Jesus' crucifixion, the risen Christ repeats this commission in John 20: "Receive the Holy Spirit. If you forgive anyone his sins, they are forgiven; if you do not forgive them they are not forgiven" (Jn 20:22-23).

This ethical responsibility of the church does not lead to the absurd conclusion that the church (or its leaders) has the right to decide who gets into heaven or not, or that it may decide that the commandment against theft or adultery is no longer relevant. But beyond the clear outlines of the will of God there lies wide scope for human ethical discernment and application. *If* the foundation of Jesus Christ and the apostles and prophets is respected and intact, *if* Jesus is truly "in the midst" of the decision makers (Mt 18:20), and *if* the Holy Spirit is present and in control (Jn 20:22), *then* the church may proceed with confidence. God will respect our earthly decisions in heaven.

The church has, for example, the freedom and responsibility to decide whether and when to remove from leadership or full fellowship an unrepentant, corrupt politician or embezzling financier or lying journalist or adulterer. And it has equal freedom and responsibility to extend full forgiveness and restoration to any of the above at the appropriate time. Church discipline (like teaching, worship, witness and all of its other functions) has often been neglected or abused. For some groups (like the ancient Pharisees) it comes much easier to "bind" and "retain sins." For others it is preferable to be as "loose" and "forgiving" as possible. Both a legalistic bondage and a careless looseness are terrible mistakes. But in faithfulness and humble dependence on God, the church, to be authentic and biblical, *must* be a disciplined community. Jesus Christ is the head of his body, the church. But there is a conversation, a give-and-take between the head and his assistants. Every decision is not dictated from the clouds. What *has* been dictated is that we in the church must bear responsibility for disciplining and forgiving one another as we proceed in our discipleship.[4]

The Great Paradox and Stumbling Block (Mt 16:21-23; Jn 6:52-71)

It would have been nice at this point if the disciples could have burst into spontaneous applause at this great vision described by their Lord and had a great feast of celebration together! But it was just at this point that Jesus began to teach his disciples more specifically the great paradox and climax of the church and the Christian faith. The Son of God, the Christ they had confessed, must suffer and die before being raised again on the third day. Their King would reign not by overwhelming all opposition with coercive power but by a love that would lead to death. He would suffer, then reign; die, then live; become last, then first. There was no other way.

The death of Christ was the great stumbling block and scandal for the original disciples and it remains so for us today. We instinctively like the victorious triumphant "Lion of the tribe of Judah"—which Jesus certainly was and is. We like following the Messiah, the King of kings, the only beloved Son of Almighty God. It does not come naturally to us to follow and worship the defeated, weak, dying and dead. It is repulsive to talk of "eating flesh" and "drinking blood" in order to live. Crucifixion, in particular, was ugly and shameful, the death not of heroes but common criminals.

So even though Jesus said clearly that he would be raised again on the third day, the paradox was too great for Peter to handle. He blurted out his rebuke and protest to Jesus as easily as he had blurted out his great confession moments earlier. His words, "Never, Lord! . . . This shall never happen to you!" sound ominously and strangely like the words of the satanic serpent in Genesis 3: "You will not surely die" (Gen 3:4). It is Satan's greatest lie to affirm that sin does not lead to death, that it is possible and desirable to pursue "the good life" in total disregard of the Word of God on the one hand and death on the other. This explains the strong rebuke Jesus gave to Peter: "Get behind me, Satan! You are a stumbling block to me; you do not have in mind the things of God but the things of men." Peter had mouthed the devil's lie.

Sin is separation from God. It is a refusal of the Source of Life, a rebellion that can only lead to death and judgment. Jesus has come into the world to set it free, to provide life. As the Lamb of God, Jesus will take on himself the sin of the world. He will take on the powers of death and defeat them by his resurrection. He will suffer vicariously for the sins of the human race and make possible their total, gracious forgiveness. Jesus cannot and will not evade the suffering and death for which he has come into the world.

In another episode, back in the synagogue at Capernaum, Jesus explained the necessity of his death by the well-known imagery of eating his flesh and drinking his blood (Jn 6:48-58). "I tell you the truth, unless you eat the flesh of the Son of Man and drink his blood, you have no life in you. Whoever eats my flesh and drinks my blood has eternal life, and I will raise him up at the last day" (Jn 6:53-54). It was a "hard saying" and "from this time many of his disciples turned back and no longer followed him" (Jn 6:66). But when Jesus asked the Twelve, "Will you also go away?" Peter (again!) replied for them, this time without reservation or mistake: "Lord, to whom shall we go? You have the words of eternal life. We believe and know that you are the Holy One of God" (Jn 6:67-69).

This is hard to handle. Unless we accept (that is, take in, internalize, "eat and drink") the sacrificed Jesus Christ, we can never have within us the means of passing through death into life. We must seize this gift by faith, invite Christ into our life and being. But just as Peter's confession of Jesus as "the Christ, the Son of the living God" came from outside "flesh and blood" human reasoning and was the revelation of God, so in the present context Jesus says, "No one can come to me unless the Father has enabled him" (Jn 6:65). No less than walking on water, it is the power of God which enables us to see clearly and accept fully the sacrifice of Jesus Christ for our redemption.

At the Heart of the Church

Clearly, there is much more to be said about the church. The leadership of the church (elders, deacons and so on), the role of the Holy Spirit (in giving gifts, guiding worship and so on) and other aspects are dealt with in Acts and the letters of the New Testament. But a decisive revelation has been given already by Jesus to Peter and the disciples. The foundation and fundamental shape and activity of the church are already apparent.

The church gives expression to the first task of discipleship: being with God in Jesus Christ in a common life together. Church experience begins when we are joined by our confession that Jesus is the Christ, the Son of the living God. Because the church is founded on Peter and the apostles and prophets, it must always build its life carefully on the Bible—the testimony of those apostles and prophets and the revelation of God. It is a community of worship (a priesthood and temple, Peter tells us), a community of witness and proclamation, and a community of mutual care, discipline and freedom.

At the very heart of the church is the person of Jesus. He is the Christ, the Son of the Living God. He is at the same time the lamb of God whose death leads to resurrection, not only for himself but for others. There are three powerful symbols of this reality which help today's churches keep alive the truth of Jesus Christ. The first is the *cross*. There is no biblical command to hang crosses in our church buildings—least of all the misleading, jeweled or "artistic" crosses which call attention to the cost and extravagance of their composition or the artistic creativity of their designers! Still, the plain, simple empty cross is a powerful reminder of the centrality of Jesus' death for the church. The fact that it is empty reminds us that the death of Christ led to the resurrection.

The second symbol is *baptism*. Baptism by water is the symbol of the disciple's conversion to Christ. The fact that it is uncomfortable (take off that three-piece suit!) and a little humiliating (my hair is messed up!) is all to the good! The purpose is to publicly declare our identification with Jesus Christ. "Death to my old self," we say symbolically as we are lowered in the water; "alive in the new life of the resurrected Christ," we say symbolically as we are lifted out of the water. It is a public declaration of our faith in Jesus Christ, our Lord, who underwent the ultimate baptism on our behalf.

The third and most important symbol is the *Lord's Supper*. This is the symbolic meal of bread and wine requested and presided over by Jesus with his disciples on the night he was betrayed. "This is my body given for you; do this in remembrance of me," he said as he broke the loaf apart and distributed it to his disciples. "Drink from it, all of you. This is my blood of the covenant," he said as he passed around the wine goblet (see Mt 26:26-29; Mk 14:22-25; Lk 22:15-20). As Paul went on to say after quoting this in his first letter to the Corinthians, "For whenever you eat this bread and drink this cup, you proclaim the Lord's death until he comes" (1 Cor 11:26). It is nothing short of a scandal in many of our churches that the Lord's Supper is so infrequently and poorly celebrated! Once a month (or less!) the Lord's Supper is "tacked on" at the end of a service in far too many congregations. But isn't this a step toward the mistake Peter made at Caesarea Philippi? Isn't this a symbolic denial of the centrality of the death of Christ for the resurrection life of the church?

It is very likely that the early church celebrated the Lord's Supper

every time they got together—or at least one time per week.[5] The fact
that some churches have "paganized" and "remythologized" the
Lord's Supper, so that it is supposed to have a concrete, "magical"
impact on those who eat, should not deter us from restoring the
memorial feast to its rightful place. The Lord's Table—not the pulpit
or choir loft—ought to be the center of our attention when we gather.
By no means are the pulpit or choir loft to be despised. We gather
to hear the word of the Lord and to present our gifts, including those
of music. But centrally, the "temple" and the new "priesthood" gather
with Jesus Christ in their midst in order to give praise and worship
to God. Even our architecture and furniture arrangements ought to
contribute to this set of priorities.

The church gathers and the church is sent out again into the world.
Just as it is gathered around the Jesus Christ of the cross, so also the
church goes out with each disciple called to take up his or her own
cross and follow Jesus through the week in daily life in the world (see
Mt 16:24-27). This means that we are called to live constantly the
"baptized life," the life of the resurrection. We are called to suffer, if
need be, in a world still under the thumb of the enemy. Peter's first
letter explains this possibility of suffering better than any other text
in Scripture. He, the one who objected to the suffering of Christ, became the greatest teacher in the Christian church of the true meaning
of the cross and suffering of Christ and of the disciple!

In our comfortable, triumphalist churches of the West we are deeply in need of church renewal centered on the Christ who died and
rose again. If our church gatherings suppress the sacrifice of Christ,
it is inevitable that the individual disciples will be unprepared and
disinclined to go out and make any personal sacrifices in the world.

Having said all of this, the last word remains *resurrection.* The way
of the cross is a *way,* not a stopping point. The goal is the righteousness, peace and joy of the kingdom of God. Death gives way to victory
for those who follow Christ. And this victory is already ours, in part,
in the resurrection of Jesus Christ and the coming of the Holy Spirit.
The gates of hell will not prevail against Jesus' work in building the
church. The spirit of Jesus Christ comes among us in special ways as
we are gathered together in the church. No disciple can "go it alone."

Being a part of the church often brings great frustrations and disappointments. But it is also one of the greatest and most promising adventures among God's gifts to us.

A footnote on choosing a church. It is, of course, a great tragedy that the Christian church is so fractured into various denominations. It is not my purpose to try to explain here all these divisions. Your expectations may be raised by this study, however, and the question may be asked, "Where can I find a church with this sort of emphasis?" Let me suggest three criteria and a strategic conclusion. First, you should only join a local church that clearly confesses Jesus Christ as Lord, Savior and God. Second, you should only join (or remain in) a local church that is intent on growing on the foundation of the apostles and prophets, in other words, that is intent on being obedient to Scripture as the Word of God. Third, if a choice is possible, you should belong to a fellowship as close to your home as possible, for the sake both of your deeper participation and the possibility of a more vigorous, united presence in your neighborhood by the church of Christ.

Strategically, the best choice is usually to stay in your present church and work humbly for reform. You have friends and relationships there that may help you in bringing about reform. If you must change churches, go to another existing church closer to home and closer to Jesus and Scripture. The most tantalizing (and deceptive) option is to start a new church with friends of like mind. But if you do not grow, you are a "holy club" and not the growing, outreaching church our Lord intended. If you grow by "stealing discontented sheep" from other churches, you are very likely undermining the chances for reform in those other "raided" churches. In any case, if you grow (as you should) you will soon have "unlike minds," and you will find over the years that most of the problems which caused you to start afresh have popped up again in your midst! It's called "human nature" and "diversity" (and perversity). By all means, start a small evening fellowship group for caring, learning, support and spiritual growth. But unless you are involved in a church-planting effort in an area totally devoid of existing churches, *beware* of perfectionist dreams. And beware of participating in the further fracturing of the universal church which belongs to Jesus Christ, not to us.

For Reflection or Discussion

1. In your own experiences in churches, what have been the high points and low points, the best and the most disappointing experiences?

2. Which of the characteristics and functions of the church described in this chapter are given most attention in your church? Which receive least attention?

3. What are some concrete ways you might help your church to become more faithful to the model intended by Jesus Christ?

6 Mountaintop & City Street: The Two Experiences

*"This is my Son, whom I love.
Listen to him!"*

IN ALDOUS HUXLEY'S BRILLIANT 1932 NOVEL, *BRAVE NEW WORLD,* ALL CITIzens of his twenty-fifth-century society are happy all the time. This is because of their genetic and social conditioning, first of all. The specially-bred human drones—the "gammas," "deltas" and "epsilons"— are just as happy doing their physical labor as the bright "betas" and super-bright "alphas." No labor is experienced as tedious or toilsome anymore. Sacrifice has no meaning since everyone is doing what their conditioning prepares them for. And, in addition, the superdrug *soma* is freely available to all classes for the perfect "high" any time it is desired. With soma, "eyes shone, cheeks were flushed, the inner light of universal benevolence broke out on every face in happy, friendly smiles."[1]

Huxley was alarmed to discover by the fifties that his nightmare had, in large part, become Western civilization's dream, toward which it was rushing much sooner than six hundred years hence. In the decade of the eighties it is clear that a kind of "soma holiday," as they

called it in *Brave New World*, has become the "kingdom of God" for
our society. We are a culture of narcissism in the grip of the myth of
happiness and immediate gratification. Toil and sacrifice are to be
avoided at all costs. Sensory "highs" and "feeling good" are the carrot
at the end of every stick. The "soma" of our era is cocaine, marijuana,
alcohol, sexual orgasm and a host of engaging distractions of all types.

As is always the case, the church is not immune from the influence
of its environment. This does not imply that Christians are simply to
pronounce a curse on the world and flee to some isolated preserve—
nor is our role that of the permanent killjoy in the society around us!
But the besetting sin of the church over the centuries is conformity
to the world. This conformity and accomodation is usually very subtle
in its beginnings but it flowers, all too often, in an outright, enthusiastic justification of the world *as it is*.

Christian disciples are called to an adventure of being holy. Here
is how Peter described this call in his first letter:

> Therefore, prepare your minds for action; be self-controlled; set
> your hope fully on the grace to be given you when Jesus Christ is
> revealed. As obedient children, do not conform to the evil desires
> you had when you lived in ignorance. But just as he who called you
> is holy, so be holy in all you do; for it is written: "Be holy, because
> I am holy." (1 Pet 1:13-16)

The root meaning of *holy* is "different" and "set apart." As in the text
above, this difference involves both thought and action. It is an adventure because in every generation we must ask again what it means
concretely in daily life to be holy, different like God. Holiness is not
a simple imitation of various "holy men" and "holy women" from the
past. Nor is it a nihilistic weirdness or eccentricity for its own sake. It
is a difference in mind and behavior out of obedience to God and
at his direction. We are holy, first of all, *for God*. But this also turns
out to be an expression of God's love *for the world*. Only by exhibiting
God's difference can we represent the creative good news of Jesus
Christ. It is no favor to the world to lull it along as it is with a reassuring Christian conformity.

So we must begin again with self-criticism and realism. Is it appropriate for the contemporary church to promote Jesus as the "best

high" available? Is the kingdom of God a glorious, unending "soma holiday?" Is the popular song true that since I met Jesus "I am happy all the time!"? Does the Holy Spirit promise to keep our soul in a state of perpetual bliss? I do not think so. Well-intended as it might be, the gospel of good feelings and a perpetual spiritual high is not true to experience or, more importantly, the Word of God. It is a Christian version of the toothpaste commercials which promise an ecstatic love life if one uses their product.

Jesus and the Holy Spirit wish fullness of joy for us, but that is not the same thing as constant bliss and happy feelings. Jesus wept. He and most of his followers for the past two thousand years could in no way be described as perpetually thrilled and happy. The Christian life *does* have its visionary highs, as we shall see. But what is to be sought is the reality of God's presence—for himself—not as a useful means of getting high. The presence of God will bring some "highs," but also some consternation and even depression—if the Psalms are any indication (and I think the Psalms are an excellent, full catalog of the movements and moods of the heart searching for God's presence).

The converse (not much of a threat to today's church) is no better. A morbid preoccupation with "what a worm am I" (Charles Wesley's fascination with our vermicular qualities in his marvelous hymns!) is not the biblical answer to our situation. At times it would seem that some Christian groups have suggested this. Unless you have on your bib overalls and suffer, your spirituality is in question. You must be somber and morose. Some of yesterday's fundamentalists and Anabaptists and today's sad-faced radical Christians could well use an ecstatic vision or two to break them out of this grumpy spiritual malaise.

The answer is the pursuit of God's presence. "Seek God's presence and the appropriate feelings will be added unto you" is how we might put it. Once again, Simon Peter provides a marvelous example of the way a disciple's pursuit of God brings with it the "two great experiences." First, accompanying Jesus to the Mount of Transfiguration, Peter had the all-time mountaintop experience from which all others derive their name! Second, back on the flatlands at dinner with Jesus, Peter was given the ultimate lesson in mundane, street-level discipleship when his Lord got down and washed his grimy feet.

The Mountaintop Experience (Mt 17:1-8; Mk 9:2-8; Lk 9:28-36)

Just one week after the episode at Caesarea Philippi, Jesus took his three most eager disciples, Peter, James and John, on a brief retreat. They climbed a high mountain together to pray. As Jesus was praying, suddenly he was "transfigured before them. His face shone like the sun, and his clothes became as white as the light." Peter, James and John had been at the point of dozing off during the prayers, perhaps because of the long climb. As they watched Jesus now, though, they also saw two other figures talking with their shining Lord. It was Moses and Elijah, the great Old Testament prophets, talking with Jesus about his coming death in Jerusalem.

As the figures of Moses and Elijah began to disappear, Peter spoke up for the first time: "Lord, it is good for us to be here. If you wish, I will put up three shelters—one for you, one for Moses and one for Elijah." (Mark's Gospel, based on Peter's recollection, adds that Peter "did not know what to say," and they were very frightened by this awesome vision.)

But while Peter was still talking, a bright cloud overshadowed them and a voice from the cloud said, "This is my Son, whom I love; with him I am well pleased. Listen to him!" When they heard this voice, the disciples fell with their faces bowed to the ground, "terrified." But then Jesus came over, touched them and said, "Get up. . . . Don't be afraid." When they got up and looked around, the vision was over. They saw only Jesus.

After this mountaintop "retreat," Peter, James and John kept quiet about the experience. Jesus asked them not to talk about it until after his resurrection. Many years later, though, as you can imagine, this experience was still clearly imprinted on Peter's mind. In his second letter, Peter stresses that "we did not follow cleverly invented stories when we told you about the power and coming of our Lord Jesus Christ, but we were eyewitnesses of his majesty. For he received honor and glory from God the Father when the voice came to him from the Majestic Glory, saying, 'This is my Son, whom I love; with him I am well pleased.' We ourselves heard this voice that came from heaven when we were with him on the sacred mountain" (2 Pet 1:16-18). Perhaps this is partly what John meant when he wrote, "We have seen his glory, the glory of the one and only Son, who came from the Father" (Jn 1:14).

Just as Peter experienced his most memorable "beatific vision" when he had drawn apart from his ordinary surroundings to the mountain, many other Christians have discovered that their most intense encounters with God come "on retreat." We need to recall that Jesus regularly, frequently, went off by himself to pray. It is certain that one can encounter the Lord in the ordinary hustle and bustle of daily life. But it is also valuable, perhaps essential, to carve out time to retreat to a place free of distractions, to seek the face of God.

For some disciples this means rising very early in the morning to be alone with God. For others it might mean backpacking or mountain climbing alone or with friends. Ironically, some of my own deepest experiences of the presence of Christ occurred while I tended machinery in a very noisy factory during the summers of my undergraduate college years. I was "apart" from the world because my job was dull, mindless physical labor, and the factory was so noisy no one could possibly communicate with anyone else! I was thus free to pray and meditate undistracted. More recently, however, I have found it helpful to go away to a place without telephone, newspapers, mail delivery, television, radio and the other distractions of my normal existence. No location will produce a vision of Christ or the voice of God as we read Scripture, pray and meditate. But location can *assist* us in quieting our lives and minds in order to listen to God.

The particular content of Peter's mountaintop experience was, in an important way, unique and unrepeatable. At the same time, we must ask what we can learn from this episode, for it remains the word of God to all disciples. God is the same; we are made out of the same stuff as Peter. We can expect that the living God will make himself known to us in powerful, moving ways. But we should not restrict, or attempt to restrict, the mode by which we see God. We should not look for a reproduction of Peter's (or any other disciple's) experience. For one reason, we should observe well the vast variety of modes by which God made himself known to the prophets and apostles. Ezekiel, Daniel and John saw spectacular, intricate images of wheels, statues, golden candlesticks and the like. David heard music and poetry in his heart. Luke heard God as he wrote a historical-theological essay. In addition to giving God a lot of room to decide how to encounter us, we must note that Peter did not specify or conjure up the form or content of his own experience here. Peter simply followed after Christ.

I have never been able to understand why Christians have felt it necessary to promote certain techniques to conjure up the presence of God. Other religions, of course, have various meditation techniques, chants, drugs and so on. The God we know in Christ is the God who comes into daily life. I think it is a mistake even for Christians to try to differentiate in the serious study of Scripture from a different kind of "devotional reading" of the Bible. At all times, not least in serious study, God can and will make himself present to us and speak his Word to us. Again, the only necessity is that we give more or less undistracted attention to the pursuit of God. All students should approach their studies this way, asking God to teach them and speak to them in the process. What is required of all of us is to follow Peter's example: make the time and exert the effort to follow and be with Jesus Christ.

The exact mode and form of Peter's experience is not normative. But the content, in general, supplies us with a kind of norm for our own mountaintop experiences.[2] The greatest of the prophets are there (Moses and Elijah, and so are the inner circle of the apostles!) but the focus is on the person of Jesus Christ. Specifically the vision centers on the death and resurrection of Christ, and then on the overwhelming declaration by God the Father himself that Jesus is his Son, well-beloved, and that it is he to whom we should listen. Whatever else may be the content of what God wishes to give us in our dreams, visions, studies, meditations and mountaintop experiences, the center must always be Jesus Christ, the risen, glorified Lord of all. No spiritual or mystical experience can be legitimate if it does not center on, and flow from, this source.

Peter's feelings during this experience are typical of those who encounter God. On the one hand he was irresistibly drawn to the presence of the Source of life and reality; on the other hand he was overcome by awe and a kind of fearful respect for the Almighty Holy One. We recall Peter's first reaction on his conversion day: "Go away from me, Lord; I am a sinful man!" All too often in our own era, this latter characteristic is soft-pedaled. Yet if God is truly present, we will simultaneously be drawn by his love, graciousness and forgiveness and be respectful of his majesty and holiness. The presence or absence of the confession of sin in personal and corporate worship is one indication of how well the holiness of God is known.

As usual, Peter made a mistake in the midst of his greatest mountaintop experience. (And we can recognize ourselves once again!) He suggested building three booths or shelters for Jesus, Moses and Elijah. His error had three aspects. First, "he did not know what to say"— but he blabbered on anyway. The proper response was silence, listening to the voice of the Lord, not chattering and activity. God's voice straightened him out in a hurry. Second, the proper focus was on Jesus Christ, not on Moses and Elijah. The role of the latter was to glorify Jesus, not compete with him for the attention of disciples. Third, Peter's mistake reflects a natural but ill-conceived desire to "capture" an extraordinary experience. Our experiences with God are existential, lived realities. The memory of them sustains us to some degree, but God intends to meet us again. The Christian life will not consist of visiting monuments to our past experiences with God!

The patience and persistence of God with his people is amazing. The voice of God breaks through in spite of Peter's enthusiastic error. This time he falls down in true worship and silence. Then the experience is over, but Jesus touches him on the shoulder, helps him up and walks down off the mountain with him side by side. Jesus is with them in the ordinary, just as he is in the extraordinary.

Peter, James and John told no one about this experience at that time. They knew there might come a time when they could refer to this experience as evidence of the identity of Jesus and in glory to God. But, ordinarily, what is gained by boasting of our past encounters with God? It might inspire jealousy, disbelief or questions about our sanity. It turns the focus to the past instead of the present. It might draw more attention to us than to the Lord we encountered. Despite the popularity of shrines to the unusual experiences of saints, despite the drama and excitement of a program of personalities telling about their most amazing close encounters with God, I suspect our Lord had later generations in mind, also, when he advised them to keep quiet about it.

Servanthood in Daily Life (Lk 22:24-30; Jn 13:1-17)

During the days and weeks following Peter's mountaintop experience, Jesus and the disciples carried on with their threefold task (see chapter one), first in Galilee, then in Samaria, and finally in Jerusalem during the week of Passover (probably in the spring of A.D. 33). The quest to heal the hurting and battle the powers which enslaved people continued. The good news of the gracious rule of God was widely disseminated and more fully elaborated by Jesus' teaching. The community of men and women responding to the call to be with Christ grew larger. *Seventy* representatives of Jesus were now sent out with the same commission as that given to the Twelve (Lk 10:1-20).

Growth in understanding was, however, tougher to come by than growth in numbers! Despite Jesus' explanations of the centrality and necessity of his death and resurrection in the great episode at Caesarea Philippi, the disciples' reaction was again "great distress" and "lack of understanding" when Jesus made his second prediction of the passion in Galilee soon after (Mt 17:22-23 and parallels). Equally difficult was the revolutionary notion that for a disciple of Jesus greatness is expressed in humility and servanthood rather than overt power, glory and ostentation. It was right after this second prediction of the passion that the disciples argued about which of them was the greatest. Jesus responded by placing a child before them as an example of humility and servanthood (Mt 18:1-5).

Normally, of course, one is a servant out of necessity or compulsion by others. One exercises leadership by ordering or persuading others to carry out servant tasks. Just at this time in Capernaum, the tax collectors came to Peter asking if Jesus was going to pay the half-shekel "temple tax" like other people (Mt 17:24-27). In the discussion provoked by this taxation, Jesus pointed out that normally the family members of a given king are free of the obligation to pay taxes; taxes are collected from other subjects. In the case of the temple, Jesus (and Peter) were in fact free of the tax obligation because they were part of the family of God, the temple family. However, "in order not to give offense," Jesus had Peter pay the tax anyway. It was a *voluntary* relinquishing of their rights, a voluntary servanthood on behalf of others.

This was an extremely difficult concept to grasp and even more difficult to practice—then, as now. But it is at the heart of Christian experience. Jesus laid down his life voluntarily for the salvation of others, even his enemies. His disciples were to voluntarily lay down their lives in the service of others. It would not be because they were slaves who *had* to do this, for they were in fact the free children of the kingdom. It would be a new way of leadership, leadership through love and voluntary, sacrificial servanthood.

All of this came to a head in the "upper room" where Jesus met with his disciples on the night of his betrayal in Jerusalem. It was just before the Passover feast. John says that "having loved his own who were in the world, [Jesus] now showed them the full extent of his love" (Jn 13:1). As the evening meal was being served, Jesus showed them the full extent of his love first in the celebration and explanation of the Lord's Supper—the bread and wine which were to be eaten and drunk in remembrance of his body and blood given for their new life (Mt 26; Mk 14; Lk 22; 1 Cor 11; John writing much later did not repeat the details of the Lord's Supper).

As the disciples sat around after eating together, incredibly, "a dispute arose among them [again] as to which of them was considered to be greatest" (Lk 22:24). Jesus "knew that the Father had put all things under his power, and that he had come from God and was returning to God; so he got up from the meal, took off his outer clothing and wrapped a towel around his waist. After that he poured water into a basin and began to wash his disciples' feet, drying them with the towel that was wrapped around him" (Jn 13:3-5). In any time and place (speaking from experience), it is a great gift to have your feet washed (and massaged, hopefully!) by someone else. In a culture where people wore sandals, walked as the normal means of transportation, and where the city streets were usually dirt—foot washing was one of the supreme acts of humble servanthood. Normally the task of a hired servant, foot washing was the task Jesus stooped to perform for his followers right after the communion meal. In the context of the Lord's Supper and the disciples' argument about greatness, Jesus' action was not only a concrete act of love but an action rich in symbolism, as he was to explain.

When Jesus came to Peter's feet, Peter resisted. "No, . . . you shall never wash my feet." Jesus responded, "Unless I wash you, you have no part with me." "Then, Lord, . . . not just my feet but my hands and my head as well," Peter said. Jesus answered, "A person who has had a bath needs only to wash his feet; his whole body is clean." When he finished, Jesus asked the disciples, "Do you understand what I have done for you? . . . You call me 'Teacher' and 'Lord,' and rightly so, for that is what I am. Now that I, your Lord and Teacher, have washed your feet, you also should wash one another's feet. I have set you an example that you should do as I have done for you. I tell you the truth, no servant is greater than his master, nor is a messenger greater than the one who sent him. Now that you know these things, you will be blessed if you do them" (Jn 13:8-17).

Another Gospel account elaborates the point further:

The kings of the Gentiles lord it over them; and those who exercise authority over them call themselves Benefactors. But you are not to be like that. Instead, the greatest among you should be like the youngest, and the one who rules like the one who serves. For who is greater, the one who is at the table or the one who serves? Is it not the one who is at the table? But I am among you as one who serves. You are those who have stood by me in my trials. And I confer on you a kingdom, just as my father conferred one on me, so that you may eat and drink at my table in my kingdom and sit on thrones, judging the twelve tribes of Israel. (Lk 22:25-30)

What is being described here is the ordinary experience of discipleship in the world. Being with Christ on the mountaintop is also a part of the disciple's experience, but it is exceptional. Being with Christ as a servant among his people is the master theme for discipleship in the footsteps of Christ.[3] It is taught over and over again by Jesus; it is equally stressed in the teaching of the apostles. The people of Christ are in the world as agents of loving service to others. We are to provide leadership by servanthood.

Christian servanthood is enclosed within the triumph and victory of the kingdom of God. Jesus "knew that the Father had put all things

under him," *so* he knelt down and washed their feet. He knew that
he was free and did not have to pay the temple tax, but he paid it
anyway so as not to offend anyone. The disciples will sit and feast at
Jesus' table in the kingdom of God. It is as the free heirs of the
kingdom that they choose to serve. In fact, the kingdom is not merely
future but is now among them; they now have eternal life. They now
may expect to be "blessed" if they do these things that Jesus calls them
to. Christian servanthood is not working *toward* power; it is working
from power. It is not a grasping for autonomy; it is an act flowing out
of their freedom. Christian servanthood is thus free, voluntary and
joyful, constrained only by the love of Jesus Christ.

Christian servanthood is also subordinated to the one great, absolute act of suffering servanthood, that of Jesus Christ's giving of his
life on the cross. In Jesus' foot-washing example for the disciples,
Peter's initial resistance gives way to a request for a total bath! In
Christian symbolism though, rooted in Jesus' teaching, the "total
bath" happens once in the disciple's life (and is symbolized by baptism); foot washing is a partial, limited service that must be repeated.
So, in reality, Jesus' great act on the cross happens once; his smaller
acts of sacrifice are repeated frequently through his disciples. Peter
has already "had a bath"—what he needs now is to have his feet
washed. He has already left all to follow Christ—what he needs now
is to be helped to rid himself of some dirt he has picked up.

At first glance it would seem that Peter has gone to the opposite
extreme from "lording it over" others since he then resisted one who
wished to serve him. On closer analysis, both attitudes have in common a desire for a kind of autonomous power and control. Thus,
Peter's resistance to Jesus' desire to voluntarily wash his feet arises out
of a kind of independence and self-sufficiency. It is very difficult to
be voluntarily served by another! It requires self-sacrificing humility
to serve, but it also requires humility to be served. It is a perversion
of discipleship to wish only to aggressively serve others, and to stand
above the need of help from others. It is difficult for many of us to
be dependent. Two examples will make this clear. With regard to
money, it is often very difficult both to part with our own and to accept
from others in time of need. With regard to what might be called

"corrective counsel" for a straying disciple, few services are more difficult to render, and few are more humbling to accept. But true servanthood is a two-way street.

Christian foot washing and servanthood, finally, must not be confused with docility and quietism. It is nothing less than Jesus' new form of leadership. Christians do not respond to violence, corruption, injustice, hunger, anxiety or any other problem of human existence by being acquiescent doormats, saying, in effect, "walk on me." Christians are called to respond, to act in the face of challenge. Only the work of Jesus Christ constitutes the absolute response of God to evil in the world. There is no "salvation" in our activities. Nevertheless, Christian servanthood represents a true, if partial, introduction of the leadership of the kingdom of God into our society. Servant leadership means leadership by example instead of imperial edict. It is concrete and specific instead of abstract and general. It is the action of love rather than coercion. It seeks to address real needs and root problems, rather than restricting itself to symptoms on the surface.

Second Thoughts on Servanthood (1 Pet)

At first, Peter may have had the most difficult time of all the disciples in understanding both the suffering and the servanthood of Jesus. But by the time he wrote his first letter, it is clear that no one understood the meaning of Christian servanthood better than Peter. He offers both a general understanding of servanthood and applications to the particulars of political, economic and marital relationships. His discussion proceeds from the concept of subordination.

"Submit yourselves for the Lord's sake to every authority instituted among men: whether to the king, as the supreme authority, or to governors" (1 Pet 2:13-14). "Slaves, submit yourselves to your masters" (2:18). "Wives, in the same way be submissive to your husbands" (3:1). "Husbands, in the same way be considerate as you live with your wives, and treat them with respect" (3:7). "Finally, all of you . . ." (3:8). Paul used the same term to refer to all Christian relationships: "Submit to one another out of reverence for Christ" (Eph 5:21). The Greek word behind these translations "submit," "be subject to," and so on, is *hupotasso*, which means literally "rank yourself under," or "assume the lower rank." Closely connected with this term is the frequent call to "respect" and "honor" others. The first move in the life of servant-hood is thus to take the place of a servant, adopt the role and style of a servant.

From *this* stance, then, Peter issues the call to "do what is right" and "do good" (1 Pet 2:12, 15, 20; 3:6, 11). Being a servant, being "subordinate" cannot mean either apathetic inactivity *or* the performance of evil (even if commanded by those to whom we subordinate ourselves). Subordination does not mean "unilateral obedience." Rather it is a stance and a style from which we do *God's* good. "Live as free [people], but do not use your freedom as a cover-up for evil; live as servants of God" (2:16). This means peacemaking; it means the exercise of sympathy and compassion; it means truth and honesty; it means active love. "Live such good lives among the pagans that, though they accuse you of doing wrong, they may see your good deeds and glorify God on the day he visits us" (2:12).

We are free people in Christ. But we choose to take the place of servants, to subordinate ourselves. And from that stance we carry out God's agenda in performing the "good," the "right" and the "loving." It is not without interest that Peter's longest presentation of this message is addressed to slaves or servants and that (unlike Paul's parallel discussions) there is no word to masters. This *may* be because Peter knew of no economic "masters" in the audience he wrote to. Maybe he found it unthinkable that a Christian would regard himself or herself as a master.[4] All Christians choose to be servants in this world (even if they have an executive title). Almost all commentators have noted this wide applicability of Peter's advice in the "servant" section (2:18-25).

In Peter's great paragraph on spiritual gifts (that is, the abilities God gives each of us—teaching, healing, caring, leading and so on), he summarizes the point as follows: "each one should use whatever gift he has received to serve others, faithfully administering God's grace in its various forms. If anyone speaks, he should do it as one speaking the very words of God. If anyone serves, he should do it with the strength God provides, so that in all things God may be praised through Jesus Christ" (1 Pet 4:10-11). Many contemporary discussions of spiritual gifts focus an inordinate amount of attention on the self: What are *my* gifts? What are not my gifts? Peter's discussion, in contrast, focuses attention on using *whatever* you have to glorify God by serving others. Our gifts and abilities are not for our aggrandizement and distinction; they are for God and for others. In any case spiritual gifts remain *God's* gifts, not our autonomous abilities, and it will only be with God's strength that we may administer them faithfully.

Peter's understanding of the meaning of servanthood is also driven home in his discussion of church leadership. "To the elders among you, I appeal . . . Be shepherds of God's flock that is under your care, serving as overseers—not because you must, but because you are willing, as God wants you to be; not greedy for money, but eager to serve; not lording it over those entrusted to you, but being examples to the flock. And when the Chief Shepherd appears, you will receive the crown of glory that will never fade away" (1 Pet 5:1-4). This is leadership through servanthood. The language of "not lording it over others" is identical with Jesus' comments about the way of the "rulers" and "great men" of the world. The point is to lead by example, not imperial edict; by servanthood, not lordship. We note again the stress on the voluntary nature of this servanthood. It is a choice to be followed willingly and eagerly, not because you must or because you're being paid. The true servant-leader does not "possess" his flock; it is always "God's flock." The model for servanthood and shepherding is Jesus Christ, the "Chief Shepherd." Again, servanthood is enclosed with the promise of "the crown of glory that will never fade away." In short: a marvelous summary of the meaning of servanthood and foot washing.

The Joy and the Pain of Servanthood

Jesus was the true, perfect servant. In fact, Peter's early sermons and prayers in Acts sometimes referred to God's "servant Jesus." God, Peter said, has "glorified his servant Jesus. You handed him over to be killed" (Acts 3:13). "When God raised up his servant, he sent him first to you to bless you by turning each of you from your wicked ways" (Acts 3:26). Jesus, the true servant, remained a servant even to the point of suffering and death. In fact, his cross was the culmination of his service. But beside this pain, Jesus found himself filled with great joy. In his "farewell discourse" Jesus said, "I have told you this so that my joy may be in you, and that your joy may be complete" (Jn 15:11). Servanthood brings with it the possibility of both joy and pain. The joy has to do with reality and with resurrection. There is a deep joy, satisfaction and contentment that comes with an intimate participation in the reality of the "way and the truth and the life." There is a limited kind of joy that comes with experience of things that are superficially pleasurable and enjoyable (a great cup of coffee in the morning, an exciting ride on a roller coaster, a generous compliment and so on). But there is a deep and lasting joy associated with the experience of seeing the truth in depth, hearing a word that is unmistakably that of God, living a way that is not self-deception or superficiality but reality itself.

For all of that, it remains true that reality itself is sometimes painful. It is resurrection that brings joy in the midst of pain. Fundamentally, this means the assurance that Jesus rose from the dead and that the power of God will raise us as well. We can approach all of life in the confidence that God will win out in the end, even if we cannot see this end in our own lifetime. However, sometimes we can see a kind of "miniresurrection" take place as our servanthood proceeds. It is an incomparable joy for the servants of God to see their modest acts of sacrificial servanthood bear fruit in new life when it did not seem possible. Thus, a husband or wife decides to persist in humble, sacrificial servanthood toward a cold and distant spouse—and may have the joy of seeing a dead marriage come back to life after many years. A teacher patiently sacrifices extra time and effort—and has the joy of seeing a troubled, rebellious student come alive. A business leader chooses to sacrifice and serve the needs of her employees instead of trying to overpower and crush them—and sees a new spirit of cooperation and commitment come to life in the whole business. A retired senior citizen sacrifices hours in listening to and caring for an unappreciative alcoholic neighbor—and sees that neighbor truly "born again" in Jesus Christ and able to win out over his addiction.

"In this," Peter says, "you greatly rejoice, though now for a little while you may have had to suffer grief in all kinds of trials" (1 Pet

1:6). You "are filled with an inexpressible and glorious joy" (1:8). You may have the joy of seeing some "miniresurrections"; you certainly will have the joy of knowing God's final resurrection and victory. Servanthood will sometimes be pleasant, sometimes painful. It is always the way of Jesus Christ in all movements of the disciple's life. Suffering must not deter the servant disciple: "Those who suffer according to God's will should commit themselves to their faithful Creator and *continue to do good*" (1 Pet 4:19).

Underneath all of the legends that have become associated with his memory, Saint Francis of Assisi seems to have exemplified the kind of discipleship we have been studying. Beginning with a determination to "follow nakedly a naked Christ" (in other words, a simple, absolute commitment to the real Jesus), Francis spent his life as a traveling proclaimer of the gospel and a special friend and healer for those afflicted with leprosy and rejected by medieval society. Francis had intense "mountaintop" visions and experiences of Jesus Christ. His ordinary life was one of determined servanthood to the point of personal pain and suffering. Yet Saint Francis always thought of himself, and carried himself, as a joyful "troubadour for the Lord." In the midst of rigorous discipleship he sang songs to God's good creation and to Jesus his Lord. Peter would have had no trouble recognizing this disciple and brother!

For Reflection or Discussion

1. Describe the most vivid, intense "vision" or encounter with God you have had. How, where and why did it happen? What did you do about it?
2. What, concretely and specifically, does it mean to "wash the feet" of a brother or sister today? What has been your experience in both "washing" and "being washed"?
3. How could the call to servanthood be applied in the arena of your work life (whether business, law, homemaking, being a student and so on)?

7 Autopsy of a Defeat: The Great Denial

*"I don't know this man
you're talking about."*

IT IS ALREADY VERY CLEAR THAT IF PETER IS AN EXAMPLE OF THE CHRIS-
tian disciple, perfection is not a prerequisite for the kingdom of God!
His failure of faith while walking on the water was mild compared
with what followed. At the moment of his greatest confession of Jesus
Christ at Caesarea Philippi, he blurted out the devilish suggestion that
Jesus did not have to die. To this, Jesus gave the stinging rebuke, "Get
behind me, Satan!" At the moment of his greatest "mountaintop experience," Peter thoughtlessly interrupted with a dumb suggestion
about building booths for Jesus, Moses and Elijah. To this, God Almighty thundered, "This is my beloved Son, listen to him!" When
Jesus washed his disciples' feet as the great lesson in servanthood, the
"prince of the apostles" made not one but two "off-the-wall" contra-
dictions to Jesus' teaching! Unfortunately, the worst was yet to come.

None of Peter's failures, however, should obscure for us the positive
side of his relationship with Jesus during those two or three years. We
recall his humble repentance at the knees of Jesus. We have to admire

his radical faith in leaving his nets and boats to follow Jesus, his reckless willingness to risk a walk on the water, and his courage in being associated with a controversial, often-despised leader. Whatever else he said, Peter's mouth articulated best and most decisively who Jesus really was: the Christ, the Son of the Living God. His determination to pursue and be with Jesus found him tracking after the Lord in the early morning and late night, climbing mountains and walking through city streets.

Peter is not perfect, for no Christian disciple is perfect. But the notion of perfection does come into play for a Christian disciple, in two ways. First, the new life and salvation that God gives us is theologically rooted in the perfection of Jesus Christ. We are acceptable in God's perfect kingdom because of the perfect sacrifice of the sinless Jesus Christ. As Peter describes it, "It was not with perishable things such as silver or gold that you were redeemed . . . but with the precious blood of Christ, a lamb without blemish or defect" (1 Pet 1:18-19).

Second, the ethical standard at which we always aim is nothing less than the perfection of God in Jesus Christ. "Be perfect, therefore, as your heavenly Father is perfect," is the bottom line to part one of Jesus' Sermon on the Mount (Mt 5:48). It is true that we fail. But when we get up off the ground, we must resume our attempt to live up to God's perfect standard. One of the most perverse (and frequent) deformations of Christian ethics is to rationalize a lower standard of behavior based on the certainty that we cannot be sinless in this life. At bottom, this "lesser of two evils" accomodation represents a lack of faith in the power of God. Our Lord was "tempted in every way, just as we are—yet was without sin" (Heb 4:15). While we will never be able to announce that in *all* points we have been perfect and without sin (far from it!), at *each* given point, in *each* particular situation, God promises the possibility of faithfully carrying out his will. In the most conflicted, messy situation, we should search for the opening God creates for faithful obedience. God brings the impossible into our experience. The full context of discipleship is the simultaneous presence of God's perfect call and God's unqualified, deep forgiveness and grace. Watering down the call to discipleship manifests a lack of faith in God's power *and* an arrested, dwarfed notion of God's grace and forgiveness. In short, *looking forward* we aim at nothing less than God's high calling in Jesus Christ; *looking backward* we give grateful thanks to God for the good that he has made possible and humbly confess the shortcomings that dogged our steps.

That is the theological and ethical context of perfection and imperfection. It remains to ask about the content, the substance, of perfection and imperfection. It is, of course, a serious tactical error to work at faithful discipleship primarily by an analysis of evil and a strategy of avoidance! A preoccupation with catalogs of sins leads to a life that is characterized by negativism, legalism, apathy (if we do nothing, maybe we won't make a mistake) and a preoccupation with the self and its "old nature." It makes God's "No" triumph over his "Yes." His judgment overshadows his grace in this negative, dwarfed version of discipleship. The Christian life is a positive task. It consists of positively seeking and carrying out God's will. Peter's summary of the meaning of servanthood was to "do the good" and "do the right" from the stance of a servant. His call was not merely to "be subordinate" and then "avoid evil."

Having said this, it remains true that the Word of God speaks clearly about the evil we must avoid while seeking the good. There are "vice lists" as well as "virtue lists" in the Bible (for example, Gal 5:19-23). So there is something to be said for a careful look at Peter's denial, its circumstances and its content. All four Gospels give this episode great attention. It is part of the Word of God; it is "useful for teaching, rebuking, correcting and training in righteousness" (2 Tim 3:16).

As evidenced by the degree of zeal in their disapproving attitudes, rebukes and disciplinary actions, some Christian disciples and churches give the impression that the "great denial" of Christ must have been when Peter used the wrong translation of the Bible. Or perhaps he ordered a beer with his pizza, or his hair was too long, or he wore an earring, liked rock and roll, drove a Mercedes, didn't recycle, voted Republican or was arrested in a demonstration at a weapons factory. Peter's greatest denial did not consist in gluttony, adultery or embezzlement. In drawing up this list (a little tongue in cheek, to be sure!), I am *by no means* suggesting that these issues are trivial or unimportant! The way we dress, our lifestyle, our sexual and financial behavior—in short, the totality of our life—is to be brought under the lordship of Christ. It is equally clear that, in addition to some things being explicitly prohibited by the Word of God (for example, adultery, drunkenness, oppression of the poor), all of our behavior must be examined in terms of its possible impact (stumbling or edifying) on others around us. What we need, however, is perspective. Peter's failure is, in fact, the great failure, the great denial. Understand this failure, and you will understand the root of all other failures needing to be avoided.

The Story of a Defeat

Jesus and his disciples spent an amazing evening together.[1] In the "upper room" of a house in Jerusalem, they had celebrated the Passover together, the meal which faithful Jews had eaten for well over a thousand years to remember God's mighty hand in delivering them out of Egypt. During this feast, Jesus had instituted, for the first time, a simple, new "ritual" meal of bread and wine which he asked his disciples to eat, then and in the future, to remember his death. The table conversation of the twelve disciples later took an abysmal dive to a petty argument about who among them might be the greatest. Jesus taught them the meaning of servanthood by getting some water and a towel and washing each one's feet. He also explained to them more fully the promise of their future life at table together in the "mansions" he was preparing for them in God's eternal kingdom. In the meantime, he explained, he would always be among them and in them by the Holy Spirit. It was essential, Jesus stressed, to remain connected with him, like a branch on a vine, so that his life would bear fruit in their experience. They would experience difficulties living in the world, but if they were united in a deep and true love for one another, and if they together strove to be one with their resurrected Lord, they would overcome all obstacles, and their joy and life would be full. Jesus then offered his great prayer to the Father on behalf of his followers (Jn 13-17). They sang a hymn together before they went out to the Mount of Olives. Jesus took Peter, James and John to the garden of Gethsemane where he agonized in prayer before being arrested by a band of soldiers led by the traitor Judas Iscariot.

Both during and after the amazing evening in the upper room, Peter and the other disciples showed that they had not fully comprehended all that Jesus was saying and doing. To Jesus' ironic suggestion that perhaps now they ought to "buy swords" and other provisions for themselves (they had just agreed with him that they lacked *nothing* when they went out on previous missions), they made the absurd (though well-intended) deduction that two swords discovered in the upper room might be helpful! Jesus cut off this profitless interchange by saying, "This is enough." He warned, "You will all fall away from me this night." But he promised that, after his resurrection, he would return and "go ahead of you into Galilee." To Peter, in particular, Jesus warned: "Simon, Simon, Satan has asked to sift you as wheat. But I have prayed for you, Simon, that your faith may not fail. And when you have turned back, strengthen your brothers" (Lk 22:31-32).

Peter's reaction to all of this was to make the bold assertion, "Lord, I am ready to go with you to prison and to death." Even though *they* all fall away because of you, I will never fall away! Jesus replied, "I tell you, Peter, before the rooster crows today, you will deny three times that you know me." Peter insisted: "Even if I must die with you, I will not deny you!" (Matthew and Mark point out in their accounts, however, that all the disciples said the same thing.)

When Jesus arrived in the garden of Gethsemane, where he would pray, he took Peter, James and John with him and said, "My soul is overwhelmed with sorrow to the point of death. Stay here and keep watch" (Mk 14:34). But as Jesus agonized in prayer about the "cup" he was about to drink on Calvary's cross, Peter, James and John fell asleep. He came to them and found them "asleep, exhausted from sorrow" and asked, "Simon, . . . are you asleep? Could you not keep watch for one hour? Watch and pray so that you will not fall into temptation. The spirit is willing, but the body is weak." A second time then, Jesus wrestled in prayer and returned to find them sleeping and "they did not know what to say to him." After the third time, Jesus said, "Are you still sleeping and resting? Enough! The hour has come.

Look, the Son of Man is betrayed into the hands of sinners. Rise! Let us go! Here comes my betrayer!"

At that, Judas and the troops charged into the garden to arrest Jesus. After the kiss of Judas identified which of them was Jesus, the soldiers laid hands on him and seized him. Peter yelled, "Lord, should we strike with the sword?" and without waiting for the answer drew his weapon (brought along from the upper room in foolish disregard of what Jesus had said about it), and landed one blow, severing the right ear of Malchus, the servant of the high priest. Jesus quickly said, "No more of this! Put your sword back in its place, for all who draw the sword will die by the sword. Do you think I cannot call on my Father and he will at once put at my disposal more than twelve legions of angels?" In his trial the next day, Jesus would say again, "My kingdom is not of this world. If it were, my servants would fight to prevent my arrest" (Jn 18:36). The *means* was wrong; the sword was "of this world." Peter's objective was wrong also. As Jesus went on to say, at his arrest, "The Scriptures must be fulfilled." "Shall I not drink the cup the Father has given me?" Jesus ended his repudiation of the sword by reaching out and healing Malchus's ear.

As the soldiers led Jesus away from the garden and took him to the house of Caiaphas, the high priest, "everyone deserted him and fled." Only Peter and one other disciple followed. Peter, at least, "followed from a distance." Arriving at the house, the guards ushered Jesus in before Caiaphas and the assembled Sanhedrin (the ruling council of priests, scribes and elders). Peter was able to get into the lower court-yard of the house, where he remained for the next hours as Jesus was inside being accused, insulted, interrogated, mocked and physically beaten.

Outside, a maid who worked for the high priest, stared at Peter and finally said, "You also were with that Nazarene, Jesus." But Peter replied, "I don't know what you're talking about. I don't know him." Peter walked out on the porch and then to the fire, where he stood warming himself in the chilly predawn air. A little later, another maid saw him and began saying to other bystanders, "This man is one of them. He was with Jesus of Nazareth." But again, Peter denied it and said with a curse, "I don't know the man." After another hour or so, one of the high priest's servants, a relative of the man whose ear Peter had cut off, challenged him, "Didn't I see you in the olive grove?" Others chimed in, "Your accent betrays you! You're a Galilean; you are one of those with him!"

Maybe Peter was overcome by fear. Maybe he could hear the angry shouts and the sickening sounds of a man being beaten inside. In any event, his response to this third challenge was to let loose a string of oaths, invoke a curse on himself and state emphatically: "Man, I don't know what you are saying! I don't know this man you're talking about!" Just as he was finishing his denial, the rooster began to crow. From where he was, "the Lord turned and looked straight at Peter. Then Peter remembered the word the Lord had spoken to him. . . . And he went outside and wept bitterly."

As morning broke, Jesus was bound and led to his trial before the Roman governor, Pilate, the Jewish king, Herod, the masses waiting outside. Within hours Jesus was nailed by his hands and feet to a wooden cross on the hill of Golgotha. "But all those who knew him . . . stood at a distance, watching these things" (Lk 23:49).

The Autopsy of a Defeat

As we examine this story, it is possible to identify several components in Peter's failure and defeat. He learned from his own mistakes. All disciples can profit by a careful study of how the "Rock" turned to "sand" in his most critical test. Peter's first mistake was to be *unprepared for the challenge* that he faced. He had been taught, but he had not listened well enough. He was warned, but he did not take it seriously enough. He underestimated the challenge. Jesus warned Peter, he prayed for him and he took him with him. But Peter still was unprepared to make it through.

There are three dimensions to the struggle Peter faced. He struggled against his old self, against other people and against the demonic powers. Becoming a Christian does not transform a person into some kind of "saint" or "angel." It launches a conflict between the old life and the new. Part of Peter's challenge that night was with himself: with his weariness and sorrow, his pride and reputation, his desire to be accepted, his temptation to give up and give in, his instinct to avoid shame and suffering. He also struggled against other people: those who opposed him, ridiculed him, accused him and threatened him. The price of their fellowship was the denial of his faith.

But Peter's struggle also had demonic proportions: "Satan will sift you." There was a cosmic battle going on which transcended the level of mere human cussedness and weakness. The "principalities and powers" can transform simple coins and paper money into the savage god "Mammon," wreaking havoc on those seduced into its worship. An otherwise noble desire to change the world can metamorphose into the god of violence, "Mars," leaving bloodshed and devastation in its wake. The political power can change from a simple organ of administration to the oppressive, totalitarian "Beast of Babylon," if we are not careful. The most malevolent demonic opponent of all, the Bible described as Satan, the "accuser," the "liar," the "deceiver," the "divider" and alienator. Peter was accused. He lied. He was deceived. He was alienated and separated from Jesus and from his own highest intentions.

So the battle against evil spirits and powers cannot be something the disciple carries on only to liberate others. It engages us personally as well.

Peter was unprepared to recognize this on the night of his great defeat, but in his letters he makes the point very clear. "Prepare your minds for action," he says (1 Pet 1:13). "Do not be surprised at the painful trial you are suffering, as though something strange were happening to you" (4:12). "Be self-controlled and alert. Your enemy the devil prowls around like a roaring lion looking for someone to devour. Resist him, standing firm in the faith" (5:8-9). "You must understand that in the last days scoffers will come" (2 Pet 3:3). "Be on your guard" (2 Pet 3:17). Peter learned the hard way the lesson of preparedness, of being ready for a battle that may take on cosmic proportions!

Peter's second great mistake was *overconfidence in himself*. It was bad enough to make the rash claim that he would never fall away but would be faithful even to prison and death. It was worse to say that he was better than the other disciples and would succeed even if they failed (Mk 14:29). A quiet determination is great. A commitment made to remain faithful is laudable. But braggadocio and overinflated self-confidence are a step toward failure. A "gentle and quiet spirit . . . is of great worth in God's sight," Peter advised all wives—but he implied as much for all disciples (1 Pet 3:4). "Be humble" (1 Pet 3:8). "Do not fear," Peter says, but answer your interrogators with "gentleness and respect" (3:14-16). "God opposes the proud but gives grace to the humble. Humble yourselves, therefore, under God's mighty hand, that he may lift you up in due time" (5:5-6). Peter is singing a different tune from that before his great defeat.

Peter's third critical error was *to fail to "watch and pray"* along with Jesus in the garden of Gethsemane. In our battles we must "watch," that is, be fully aware of what is happening around us and in us. And we must "pray," that is, invoke the presence, power and guidance of God in our situation. Peter was sleepy—a good excuse; the "flesh is weak"—it was the middle of an exhausting night. But Jesus won his battle. He was faithful to the will of his Father through the ultimate test. He watched and prayed through the night; Peter slept and lost. "The eyes of the Lord are on the righteous, and his ears are attentive to their prayers," Peter wrote later, quoting Psalm 34 (1 Pet 3:12). "Be clear minded and self-controlled so that you can pray" (1 Pet 4:7). Watch and pray.

The fourth mistake was to try to fight the battle with *the wrong weapons*. Peter brought along a sword to the garden—he had *never* worn one before in all of his great missions for the kingdom of God! The logic that says "we will stockpile these weapons but not use them" will find no support in Peter's experience! He had a sword with him, and in his weak moment used it. It was a spiritual battle, but he tried to use a "carnal weapon" (see Eph 6:10-18 for Paul's description of Christian warfare). The disavowal of violence is not made out of weakness but strength. Jesus could crush his enemies if he wanted, with hosts of angels if need be. But his kingdom is "not *of* this world"—even though it is *in* the world. What is true of violence may be said for deception, as well, or for any weapon "of the world." In his first letter Peter says that through faith we are "shielded by God's power" (1:5). "Do not repay evil with evil or insult with insult, but with blessing" (3:9). "Arm yourselves also with the same attitude" as Christ

(4:1). "Resist [the devil], standing firm in the faith" (5:9). The true weapons are faith, hope and love; the Word of God and the Spirit of God; servanthood and the creative alternatives provided by God's Spirit.

⑤ **Fifth,** Peter *"followed at a distance."* He became isolated and much more vulnerable as a result. This "distance" has to do with his relationship to Jesus. He tagged along at a distance. He stayed outside in the courtyard while Jesus was on trial inside. Could he have followed Jesus into his trial room? The "other disciple" may have gone in since he had acquaintance with the high priest somehow. Maybe Peter could have gone in, at risk of also being implicated in the trial. Maybe he had already blown his chance of doing this with the sword incident. At any rate, he stationed himself "at a distance" from Jesus. But, he was by this time also distanced from the other disciples with whom together he might have held faithful. Could their frequent spokesman, Peter, have rallied them to stay together? Did he try? But this point of weakness must not be charged merely (or mainly) to Peter alone. Where were his fellow disciples when he (and Jesus still more) could have used their support? They allowed Peter to go on his own—and fall on his own.

Christian discipleship is *impossible* for the isolated follower of Jesus. It was never intended that a lone disciple could live out the Sermon on the Mount or any other challenge. "Above all," Peter wrote later, "love each other deeply" (1 Pet 4:8). Peter's defeat teaches us to stay close to Jesus Christ and stay close to our brothers and sisters. Don't just watch as your fellow disciples go off alone into a situation of great risk to their faith. Follow them, love them and care for them! If your faith is at stake, ask others to come with you.

⑥ Peter's sixth mistake was to *draw close to the enemy*. He was not merely distanced from Jesus and the disciples, he was warming himself by the fires of the opposition. He stood there, sat there, and watched what was happening from the rooting section of the opposing team. Now it is very clear that Jesus and his followers were often in the company of pagans and even declared enemies of the kingdom of God. The followers of John the Baptist were upset that Jesus and his friends "ate and drank with publicans and sinners." The critical difference was that, while Jesus was "in" and "among" these groups, he was not "of" them. His words and actions bore witness, in ways either subtle or spectacular, to the grace and truth of God. Unfortunately, in Peter's case he was both "in" and "of" the crowd in the courtyard. In fact he tried very hard to merge into the crowd.

Real growth and strength can take place deep in enemy territory, but *only* if we are there as conscious, alert representatives of our Lord. Be there—but be there as an "alien and stranger," as a member of "a holy nation, a people belonging to God" (1 Pet 2:9-12). Any other "presence" in the world puts in jeopardy one's faithfulness.

Seventh, and finally, Peter failed by being too *concerned about himself.* He needed sleep in the garden. He wanted to be warm by the enemy's fire. Inside, Jesus was undergoing a vicious miscarriage of justice. Outside, Peter was taking care of himself. Inside, Jesus was being grilled about his identity and punished for telling the truth. Outside Peter was guarding his own identity to avoid the discomfort of accusation. The great commandment, Jesus said, was to "love the Lord your God with all your heart, mind, strength, and soul," and then to "love your neighbor as yourself." Peter inverted the command and willed to love himself above all, at that moment. Peter's letters many years later would stress, from beginning to end, the priority that must be given to loving and obeying God first, and then others, even at the cost of extreme discomfort to the self.

With these seven fateful steps, Peter walked over the edge of the cliff. His denial was implicit at some stages of the process, explicit at others. It culminated in the great sin of denying his relationship to Jesus Christ. He insisted three times, over several hours, that he had no connection with Jesus. Conversion had meant, fundamentally, coming into personal relationship with Jesus as Lord. Discipleship had meant being "with Christ" (he denied that he was one of those with Christ). It meant proclaiming the good news of the kingdom (he spoke denials and curses). And it meant healing and exorcism (he gave in to the devil and hacked off a man's ear). The church is founded on the confession of who Jesus Christ is. Everything turns on who Jesus is and on our relationship to him. Faith is "seizing onto" Jesus, clinging to him, depending on his work. Peter disowns and rejects Jesus; he pushes himself away.

All of our failures and shortcomings can only be designated as such because they represent a denial of Jesus Christ our Lord. Christians do not live in relation to an abstract moral code but a living Lord. When we sin economically, sexually or any other way, it is not so much that we break the rules as that we "break the heart" of the God who knows us, loves us and wills for us a way of thinking, speaking and acting that leads to life rather than death. More than violating a command, we have violated the Commander whose Word is a gracious gift. Our failures are such because they are *a breach in the faith* and confidence which binds us to our Lord. They are a concession to despair and the world as it exists, *an abandonment of the hope* and the promise linking us to God's new future. They are a *betrayal of the love* which God has lavished on us and which he wishes to extend through us to others. Everything depends on who Jesus is and on our relationship to him. The worst possible failure is to deny him and our relationship to him.

Already, this saga of Peter's great defeat puts us in question. At each of his seven fatal steps, we ought to engage in careful self-examination in hopes of avoiding his mistakes. Peter is going to recover, and that is a side of the saga not to be missed. Just as his Lord's death would be the most abysmal news in history without the resurrection, Peter's story would be extremely discouraging if not for his recovery. Peter is going to rise from the "agony of defeat" to the "thrill of victory." The first word and the last word in Peter's history is *hope*.

There is one additional footnote to be registered on this otherwise sad story. Peter, as he discovered, had lived a life that made it impossible for himself to shake the accusation that he was a follower of Jesus Christ! There was too much public evidence against him. If he had been more careful to keep his distance from Jesus in Galilee (or among the band of disciples), if he had just polished up his accent and social style so that he could have been just "one of the guys" that difficult night—then he might have slipped by unchallenged.

There is something worse than failing, and that is not even trying. Despite his radical failure, Peter was inextricably associated with Jesus Christ. It was too late to go back. The people knew it. He discovered it. For modern disciples the question needs to be asked whether our family, friends, neighbors and coworkers have a clear notion of our relationship to Jesus. The issue is not whether we are religious, or solid church members. Those associations can be maintained with at least a minimum of dignity, if not social pride! The issue is whether *Jesus* has "existential" importance in our lives. Does the living God have a firm grip on our lives throughout our daily existence? If he does, it will show itself, with or without the aid of bumper stickers, fish pins and "Jesus Saves" tie tacks.

The "autopsy" of Peter's defeat is not, then, an autopsy of Peter! He has made a laudable, enthusiastic attempt to follow Jesus in the most difficult of circumstances. He has blown it and failed miserably. But he will get up again off the ground and try again. We should do as much.

For Reflection or Discussion

1. What, in your mind, are the worst (or most frequent) forms of evil and denial of Jesus Christ in our own era? Are there forms of corporate, institutional denial along with the better-known individual, personal phenomena? Explain.

2. Have you ever been in a situation where it was embarrassing, painful or costly to be identified as a follower of Christ? When, how and why did this occur? How did you respond?

3. How can we better detect when a fellow Christian is getting into deep water and is in danger of a great failure? What practical course of action can be taken to intervene? Have you had any "intervention" experiences like this?

8 Prescription for Recovery: Peter's Stunning Comeback

"Peter, standing with the eleven, lifted up his voice and addressed the crowd."

WORD TRAVELED FROM PERSON TO PERSON LIKE WILDFIRE EARLY ON THE morning of the day of Pentecost: "Something strange and incredible is happening down on the plaza." First dozens, then hundreds of Jerusalem's residents and visitors swept down the streets to see and hear for themselves. The swelling crowd was restless. At the front of the crowd a small group of people were busily speaking to various listeners about the mighty works of God. Incredibly, it seemed, they were speaking to various foreign visitors in their own native languages! Many in the crowd were amazed and bewildered. "Aren't these the Galileans?" some shouted out. Others screamed, "They're all just drunk!" and mocked them.

As the crowd grew larger and more agitated, one of the figures causing the commotion stood up where he could be seen and heard by everyone and motioned for quiet. It was a fisherman from the village of Bethsaida, known to his friends by his nickname "the Rock." With the fires of truth and compassion burning in his heart and eyes, he then delivered the most courageous, brilliant and powerful message of his life. The audience was "cut to the heart," and almost three thousand people became followers of Jesus Christ that day. It was exactly seven weeks after the death of Christ in that same city. It was just seven weeks after that same "Rock" had fallen apart and repudiated his Lord publicly at his most critical time of need.

Naturally, there was great joy and celebration that Pentecost evening among the men and women who had remained Jesus' followers through the bleak experiences of their recent past. Not least in their joy, I am certain, would be the tearful hugs they would give to "the Rock." Peter's comeback was complete. He had been a tower of strength in that dangerous crowd of listeners, a solid rock on which God's Spirit had built three thousand new disciples into the household of God.

How did it happen? How did Peter recover from his colossal failure? Of everything said about or by Peter in the New Testament, I find this seven-week transition from defeat to victory the most moving, inspiring and even endearing of all. I love Peter, my brother and "mentor," most of all because, at this lowest, most miserable point, he got up off the ground and came back. Comeback is possible for losers and failures. Peter shows us the way.

The Christian life, we have already seen, is a struggle. One of the truest sentences ever uttered by our Lord was this: "In this world you will have trouble" (Jn 16:33). (Equally true, and much more hopeful, was what Jesus then added: "But take heart! I have overcome the world.") Discipleship is a combat, a wrestling, a warfare. This war is not without its lulls and breaks, of course. The intensity rises and falls. But the final cessation of hostilities only comes at the end, when Satan is eliminated, and when the last vestiges of our old rebellious nature are purged. In the meantime, the battle continues.

On the one hand, it is to be regretted that we must struggle. It is painful, frustrating, threatening, upsetting and depressing. Victories are temporary. Losses are costly. The struggle itself is often far from exhilarating and enjoyable. On the other hand, there are at least two redeeming features to this Christian struggle. First, our struggles really count for the kingdom of God. We really can roll back the forces of darkness in given situations, with God's help. The struggle is not merely a game whose outcome would be only as important as the players decide they want to make it. It is life, reality and history in which we are participating.

But second, struggles have a certain value for the participants themselves. It is tension and opposition that builds strength. Muscular strength is developed by "resistance training"—pushing against heavy obstacles. Character in children is developed partly by parents resisting the will of the child. Intellectual strength is developed by submitting to critical interaction with other minds, not by staying off in a corner with only those who agree with you. Community strength is not developed by a conflict-free floating along but by the alternating cycle of vigorous "give-and-take" with resolute cultivation of the common center. For body, mind and spirit, it is this kind of tension that is indispensable, though painful, for the building of character.

Peter's struggles, his defeats as well as victories, built his character. He emerged from his worst defeat at a new peak of strength. While he was busy denying and betraying Christ around enemy fires, it was difficult to see how he would ever fulfill Jesus' promise to "return" and "strengthen his brothers and sisters." But it happened. In the face of our worst struggles and failures we may take hope. Peter means hope.

Before studying Peter's recovery, we ought to reflect on our own situation. How do we deal with failure in ourselves? How do we deal with others who fail? One popular strategy is to ignore it. Don't talk about it. Pretend it doesn't exist. Run away from it. Three examples: In the thirties, Christians became aware that a Nazi doctor in their German Lutheran church was participating in some frightening human experiments at a nearby detention camp—but it was easier to ignore it than bring it up. Fifty years later, a staunchly antifascist American Christian elder in a church abandons his wife and children for the arms of another woman in his church, moving with his new wife to another church two miles away, where he is warmly welcomed and elected an elder within a year. Finally, perhaps even closer to home, we may suspect that an ill-conceived sarcastic comment has hurt a brother or sister, but we just avoid talking with him or her for the next few weeks till it blows over. Peter did not recover—nor will anyone else—by ignoring his failure.

Another option, of course, is "therapy." On the most cynical reading (justified by plenty of evidence), the counselor or therapist may help an offender to regard the failure as a kind of illness or maladjustment, rather than as a guilt-producing sin. If there is any fault to be assigned, it might be attributed to our parents—or perhaps to society! Certainly, there *are* many fine counselors and psychologists who take both evil and personal responsibility seriously and who help their clients to face up to reality. But the tragic fact is that others are assisting in a process of justification and avoidance.

No better than either of the above is what I would call the "Judas procedure." As you recall, all of the twelve disciples failed in the clutch. Two, Peter and Judas Iscariot, were spectacular disasters. Peter recovered; Judas did not. Now Judas had been called and trained by Jesus just like the others. He had all the advantages of the others. He knew and saw Jesus. He heard Jesus' teaching about Mammon and its powers. But when tempted, he agreed to betray his Lord for thirty pieces of silver. He collaborated with the enemy not just impulsively but with premeditation. Peter slid into his pit; Judas looked at his and deliberately jumped in.

Still, what Judas did after his failure could not lead to recovery but to final defeat. He repented and brought the money back to the enemy, saying, "I have sinned, for I have betrayed innocent blood." They replied, "What is that to us? That's your responsibility." Judas threw down the money, stormed out and hanged himself (Mt 27:3-10; Acts 1:16-20). Judas was remorseful and regretful—but to the enemy; he repented—but not to the Lord. He went out and committed the ultimate act of vengeance against himself and God. He murdered one of God's creatures, one of Jesus' disciples: himself. Judas died not a heroic death but a rebellious, self-centered, punitive suicide.

The "Judas procedure" is thus, to punish and destroy rather than to heal and restore. If some of the defeated ignore or justify their failures, others follow an equally unproductive course of self-flagellation and self-punishment. They are often encouraged or assisted in this rejecting-punitive process by hard-nosed zealots only too eager to hang the scarlet letter on others. Without an ounce of Christ's compassion in their hearts, without a cell of Christ's mind in their skulls, they would consign all failures to perpetual suffering, banished forever from the service of the Lord. This "Judas procedure" is as treasonous to the grace of Jesus Christ as the man for whom it is named.

When Peter's faith failed while walking on the water, Jesus reached out his hand—to rescue him, not to club him! After Peter disrupted the mountaintop experience with his inane suggestion and was silenced by God, Jesus again touched the prostrate disciple on the ground and said, "Rise, have no fear"—he did not slap him around. The prescription for recovery cannot be punitive and vindictive any more than it can consist of ignoring and avoiding the problem. There is still another road to be explored.

Peter's Road to Recovery

Immediately on hearing the rooster crow and seeing the Lord turn to look at him silently, "Peter went out and wept bitterly." He did not rush out to find the other ten cowards and rip them apart for failing to be with him. He did not justify himself by explaining how difficult his circumstances were. He was devastated by his weakness and failure and wept bitterly. It is a reasonable assumption that Peter, later that day, stood among the other acquaintances of Jesus from Galilee and sadly watched the horrors of his Lord's crucifixion.

Two days later, early in the morning before dawn, Mary of Magdala and some other women went to the tomb loaned by Joseph of Arimathea for the burial of Jesus' body. The stone was rolled away and the tomb was empty! Two angels appeared, assuring them that Jesus had risen from the dead. On the way back to the disciples with the great news, Jesus briefly encountered the women. When Peter and John heard this they sprinted back to the tomb, where Peter went in first and saw the burial garments, but no Jesus. Perplexed, they returned to their quarters. But some time during the day, Jesus showed himself to Peter (see Lk 24:34; 1 Cor 15:5).

As all the disciples were huddled together in Jerusalem that evening, Jesus surprised everyone by coming and standing among them. He showed them the wounds in his hands and feet and said, "Peace be with you." The disciples were, naturally, overjoyed to see their resurrected Lord. As they ate together, he taught them again from the Scriptures about what he had accomplished by his death and resurrection. He recommissioned them to be his representatives in the world and to have the responsibility to "forgive or retain sins," that is, to "bind and loose" in their community. He charged them to "receive the Holy Spirit" and told them that shortly the Spirit would descend on them in a powerful way.

All of this constitutes "stage one" of Peter's recovery. Quite likely, Peter felt like hanging himself—but he didn't do it. He might have been tempted to drown his misery in company with the enemy down at the nearest tavern—but he didn't. Instead, he *remembered* his rash words. He *wept* about his failure. He kept *quiet*. (Let Thomas and the others do the talking now!) He *pursued* Jesus—or the possibility of seeing Jesus (ran to the tomb, entered it first). And he *stayed among his fellow disciples* (embarrassed or not). This is only the first stage of recovery, but it is critical. It bears a striking resemblance to the first four of Jesus' Beatitudes in the Sermon on the Mount—precisely the four that are essential for the disciple's relationship to God (Mt 5:3-6; the last four Beatitudes outline the disciple's relationship to others).

"Blessed are the poor in spirit, for theirs is the kingdom of heaven." Peter's recovery began the moment he "remembered" and "recognized" his failure and poverty. "Blessed are those who mourn, for they will be comforted." Peter not only recognized his poverty, he mourned it. He wept bitterly. It really matters when we have failed God, when we have disobeyed our Lord. If our failures do not deeply trouble us, we are taking either ourselves or God too lightly. If we do not mourn, we cannot be comforted by God. If we do not mourn our poverty and failure, we cannot truly recover from our defeat.

"Blessed are the meek, for they will inherit the earth." It is not to the loud and the proud that the promise and the inheritance come; it is to the meek, that is, the humble and gentle who are dependent on God. It is what we *don't* read about Peter during these days and weeks that is decisive here. In strong contrast to his typical behavior up to the great denial, he is now quiet. It is now Thomas who throws out the daring question, not Peter. Jesus appears to the disciples—but Peter makes no statements, puts no questions on the floor. Apologies, words of repentance, explanations—fine, but those who fail ought to assume a posture of meekness and quietness, and those around them ought to recognize the importance of this quiet remembering and meditation.

"Blessed are those who hunger and thirst for righteousness, for they will be filled." Peter hungered and thirsted for the Righteous One, Jesus Christ. Out of his poverty of spirit, remorse and meekness, he pursued God and found him. The first resurrection appearance to one of the Twelve came to a humbled, fallen man who wanted badly to see Jesus again.

Equally to be noted, Peter stayed in the *community* of the Righteous One. Often when we fail our tendency is to run away. We fear the disapproval or rejection of our fellow disciples. We are deeply ashamed about our letting them down, our failing to live up to their expectations and needs.

It is extremely important to observe that there is no suggestion that the disciples rebuked or castigated this humbled brother in their midst. They didn't ask him to preach (just yet)—but they did not accuse him either. They, too, had failed in their own ways. They could see that Peter was poor in spirit, and it would achieve nothing to add their reproof to his misery. It was a community of repentance and recovery. Peter was allowed to shuffle about in quietness in their company, without any scarlet letters hung around his neck. Our churches today could often use a generous dose of this healing spirit.

After these first steps during the week following the resurrection, "stage two" in Peter's recovery took place (Jn 21). Peter and the disciples had returned to their home base in Galilee. They remembered Christ's promise that he would go before them and see them again in Galilee. Peter, John, James, Thomas, Nathaniel and two other disciples decided to take the boat out and try to do some fishing. It was an unproductive night, and they caught nothing.

Nets pulled in, their boat made its way back home just as day was breaking. When they were about one hundred yards from shore, a lone figure called out, "Children, have you any fish?" They yelled back, "No." The still unrecognizable man on the shore said, "Cast the net on the right side of the boat and you will find some." They did

so, perhaps thinking it was Zebedee who called them "children," and
who knew these waters well enough to give an order like that.[1]

The quantity of fish in their net was suddenly enormous, and they
were unable to haul it into the boat. Wheels turned in their memories.
John said to Peter, "It is the Lord!" Leaving the other six to struggle
in the boat, dragging the net to shore, Peter suddenly dove in and
made his way to where Jesus was. Jesus made a fire and served them
a breakfast of bread and broiled fish as they were all reunited on the
beach.

After breakfast, Jesus turned to Peter and asked quietly, "Simon, do
you love me more than these?" Peter replied, "Yes, Lord, you know
that I love you." Jesus said, "Feed my lambs." Jesus asked a second
time then, "Simon, do you truly love me?" Again Peter responded,
"Yes, Lord, you know that I love you." And Jesus said, "Take care of
my sheep." On the third request, "Simon, do you love me?" Peter "was
hurt" and said, "Lord, you know all things; you know that I love you!"
Jesus replied, "Feed my sheep."

"I tell you the truth, when you were younger you dressed yourself
and went where you wanted; but when you are old, you will stretch
out your hands, and someone else will dress you and lead you
where you do not want to go." (Jesus said this to indicate the kind
of death by which Peter would glorify God.) Then he said to him,
"follow me!" (Jn 21:15-19)

"Stage one" was the context and presupposition for this second stage
of Peter's stunning recovery. For full recovery to occur, it is necessary
for a disciple to *face clearly and fully* the reality of his or her failure
before the Lord. The *specifics* of the problem have to be dealt with in
all honesty and candor.

Peter was no longer the brash leader of the Twelve. He was once
again just "Simon," an ordinary fisherman into whose life and work
Jesus intervened in an amazing way. Many scholars have found it
hard to believe that a miraculous catch of fish happened *once* in
Simon's experience, let alone twice, and consider this a crude embel-
lishment of John's Gospel by a later editor. On the contrary, this story
parallel to Peter's conversion illustrates with great precision and fidel-
ity the way God often works in human lives. Many disciples expe-

rience this kind of re-entry of the Lord into their lives after growing cold, proud and losing their first love. If the nosedive is followed by repentance, quiet, fellowship, and a hungering and thirsting to encounter the Lord again, that same Jesus we knew in such power earlier in our life will suddenly press his way back in. There is a kind of recapitulation of our earlier encounter with Christ. To get back on track, we often have to go back to the beginning.

The "pedagogy" of Jesus in this situation is extraordinary (church disciplinarians take note!). Jesus deals precisely with Peter's failure. But he does not frontally assault him with: "Simon, you said you were better than your colleagues! But LOOK WHAT YOU DID! You said you would stick with me to prison and death! You thought you knew better than me, didn't you! You didn't deny me once, or twice, but THREE TIMES! And with cursing and swearing! Simon, WHAT'S WRONG WITH YOU?" This sounds all too familiar, but it is the voice of pagan leadership, not that of the Lord of hope and forgiveness.

Jesus does not directly charge Peter with a threefold denial. He effectively makes his point by asking his question three times in a row: "Do you love me more than these?" Peter refuses to say he is better than, or loves Jesus more than, the others. When Jesus poses the question, Peter says each time, "Lord, you know." No longer will he argue with Jesus that he, Peter, knows better. The first two times, Jesus asks about Peter's love using the Greek word *agape*, meaning a sacrificial, altruistic, unconditional love. In each of Peter's replies (and in Jesus' third phrasing of the question), the word that is used is *phileo*, which normally meant a somewhat more modest, reciprocal, brotherly love. Some scholars have pointed out that the usage of this vocabulary is not that precise (especially in John's writings) and that the words are essentially interchangeable. I'm inclined to believe, however, that the author of the report *was* trying to convey the dynamics of the conversation as it occurred. Peter, on this reading, refused to claim that his love measured up to this noblest, highest form of self-sacrificial giving.[2]

To each of Peter's modest but earnest confessions of his love for Jesus, the Lord responds with a commission. Peter is three times given the confidence of his Lord in the hopeful task of feeding and caring for his flock of followers. After warning Peter that he would himself one day meet with imprisonment and death, Jesus remobilized his disciple with his original and permanent challenge: "Follow me!" At the end of "stage two" Peter is up and moving again in the footsteps of his Lord.

Recovery, for Peter and for any disciple, does not mean perfection! As they rose to leave, Peter asks Jesus, "What about him?" in reference to John. Jesus rebukes Peter mildly, "What is that to you? You must follow me." This footnote on stage two demonstrates that even a humbled, recovering disciple is not free of his "old nature." He is not transformed into an "angel." There are weaknesses even during the recovery—these do not cancel out the value or significance of the great work God is doing in a life being put together again. Keep moving! Follow Jesus.

Two Trial Performances (Acts 1—2)

The third and final phase of recovery occurs when we actually resume our daily service of God, when we begin again doing the work that we are called to do.[3] About a month later, Jesus ascended back to heaven, and the disciples were left waiting for the promised Holy Spirit. With one mind, the disciples continued to pray together. Peter's first test, his "trial performance," occurred as he rose to speak to about one hundred and twenty brothers and sisters gathered together in an upper room in Jerusalem. The last time he had spoken in an upper room with his brothers and sisters, he had objected to his Lord washing his feet and had boasted that his loyalty was deeper than anyone else's! But Peter's failure had been forgiven, his chains had been "loosed," and he was now free to rise and speak. Nobody shouted him down or reminded him of his past; he was free again in the eyes of the community of faith. But how would he do? What would he say?

In a few modest but decisive sentences Peter showed that it was important to choose another disciple to make up for the loss of Judas Iscariot. As his Lord had done so often, Peter based his short plea on the Word of God. (Perhaps Peter spent a good deal of his time in studying the Scripture over the previous six or seven weeks; he was about to begin a preaching career, showing a marvelous knowledge of the Bible.) Peter's suggestion won the consent of the others and, after prayer, the decision was made to appoint Matthias to the open slot. Peter passed his first recovery test by providing admirable internal leadership in the community of faith.

The second and more important test was on the day of Pentecost in the episode described at the beginning of this chapter. Confronted by a large crowd which included angry, mocking antagonists along with the curious and awestruck, how would Peter react? As he heard the cries identifying them as "Galileans," he might have been chilled to remember the last time he had been identified as such. A similar crowd in this same city had only seven weeks earlier crucified Jesus in a public frenzy, with the full support of the police and political and religious leaders. This was the final trial in Peter's recovery. As we have noted, he passed with flying colors. Peter was back—all the way.

Peter's stunning recovery was not fully complete until he passed these two tests in relation to his servant leadership within the community and his public proclamation of Christ in a hostile world. Many years later, John would write, on behalf of the Lord, to his home church in Ephesus, "I hold this against you: You have forsaken your first love. Remember the height from which you have fallen! Repent and do the things you did at first" (Rev 2:4-5). Remember, repent, rekindle your first love, and recommence the works you used to do. What was required for the recovery of a fallen church was nothing more or less than that required of Peter in his recovery.

"Doing the things you used to do" calls for some discernment, of course. In Peter's case, Malchus's ear was healed and Jesus was risen from the dead. There were no "skeletons in the closet," no victims of his failure lying bleeding on the edge of his Pentecost audience. Given Peter's faithfulness in the movements toward recovery, given the work of Christ face to face with him, and given the power of the Holy Spirit, seven weeks was enough time for Peter's great recovery. In other cases, however, it may be that our failures leave such wreckage in their wake that a sudden return to a role as a *public* leader is premature. A premature move like this may be a scandal to the world and a painful stumbling block to the church.

The prescription for recovery remains intact, however. A public school teacher who is defeated in an ugly, wrenching marital disaster, for example, and cannot rebuild what has been destroyed, could in time recommence a quieter, nonpublic teaching ministry of great value for the kingdom of God. No one should believe that being an admired speaker to great crowds is one whit more important than working in obscurity with three or twelve young disciples (for which we have a well-known predecessor!). Do the works you did at the first. Exercise the gifts God has given you.

If you are going to suffer, Peter said later on his first letter, it is much better to suffer for doing good, for being faithful to Christ, than for doing evil and bringing it on yourself! Even so, there is no hint in Peter's mature reflections that his readers are beyond failure. "Rid yourselves of all malice and all deceit, hypocrisy, envy and slander of every kind," he counsels (1 Pet 2:1). In our struggles to "be holy as God is holy" we may fall. But if we humble ourselves under God's mighty hand, he will lift us up at the proper time. Nobody knew that from experience better than Peter, whose great defeat was followed, in due time, by a truly stunning comeback. God has not changed.

For Reflection or Discussion

1. Of the various stages and steps to recovery described in this chapter, which are the most difficult in your opinion? Why?

2. What can be done, concretely and specifically, in your local congregation to become (or prepare to become) a truly "healing" community for those who fall in various ways?

3. What other "comeback stories" do you know (in the Bible or history or recent experience)?

9 Charismatic Witness: Evangelism and Apologetics

*"Always be prepared to give an answer
to everyone who asks you to give the
reason for the hope that you have."*

WITH PETER'S GREAT COMEBACK, HIS RESTORATION AND RECOVERY, HE
was once again oriented to the three tasks of Christian discipleship.
In the preceding chapter we gave our attention to the re-establish-
ment of Peter's relationship with Jesus Christ and with the other
disciples. The Christian community met together "with one accord"
for prayer and the guidance of Scripture. Matthias was chosen to fill
the vacant apostle's position. Jesus ascended back to heaven, but the
Holy Spirit came to live in and among the disciples. Not only in the
first chapter of Acts but as a recurring theme, the building of a common life in relationship to God looms large in the story of discipleship
after Jesus' ascension. This "first task" of Christian discipleship is the
essential prerequisite for carrying out the remaining two. It is this
community which prepares and supports the disciples in their outreach to a hurting world.

The last words of Jesus before his ascension reinforced the ongoing commission: "You will be my witnesses in Jerusalem, and in all
Judea and Samaria, and to the ends of the earth" (Acts 1:8). The being
and character of the community itself constituted an important ele-

ment in that witness. But from Peter's sermon in Acts 2 onward, proclamation of the good news was aggressively carried forward (the "second task" of discipleship). And beginning with the healing of the crippled man by the temple gate in Acts 3, Peter and the disciples carried forward their mission to heal and to combat the demonic powers (the "third task" of discipleship). We will return to an examination of the shape of this "third task" in the next chapter.

Here we must take a careful look at Peter's proclamation in Acts, his evangelism and apologetics. In his first letter, written some thirty-five years after Pentecost, Peter said that a primary purpose of God's pilgrim people is to "declare the praises of him who called you out of darkness into his wonderful light" (1 Pet 2:9). So, too, he wrote, "Always be prepared to give an answer [make an apologia, defense] to everyone who asks you to give the reason for the hope that you have" (1 Pet 3:15). We have the good fortune to be able to examine how Peter himself carried out these tasks in five different messages reported in Acts (2:14-40; 3:12-26; 4:8-20; 5:29-32; 10:34-43). We will need to think of this in relation, of course, to the earlier studies of Peter's conversion (chapter one) and to the tasks of discipleship (chapter two).

In our own generation, great energy has been devoted to evangelism. Many churches are bulging with new members. There has been a rapid growth of church task forces and parachurch organizations dedicated to the task of proclaiming the gospel to people. How do these evangelistic movements approach this task? Consider five popular approaches, each of which is simply the most visible representative of a particular strategy.

Campus Crusade for Christ seeks conversions through the person-to-person presentation of a brief summary of the gospel in the form of "Four Spiritual Laws," followed by an invitation to pray to "receive Christ." During my junior year as a student at the University of California in Berkeley, an intensive campaign was carried out to present the "Laws" and invite a decision over the telephone to all twenty-eight thousand of us students! Noontime concerts and testimonies, a magic show, a speech or two from the steps of Sproul Hall, a great deal of one-on-one personal conversation, and a climactic rally in the Greek

Theatre with Billy Graham, supported this effort. In more recent years similar campaigns in various locales have made the slogans "Here's Life" and "I Found It" widely known.

Billy Graham has specialized in massive crusades in various auditoriums and stadiums around the world. Graham preaches, choirs sing, famous people give testimonies, and people are urged to get up out of their seats and walk to the front of the platform to express their conversion to Christ. Counselors move in, packets of literature are distributed, prayers are said, and local churches are involved in the follow-up of these converts.

As a third example, consider the growing presence of "televangelism." Billy Graham specials are part of this phenomenon, but the daily or weekly shows featuring the "700 Club," the "PTL Club," Jimmy Swaggart, Jerry Falwell and others are more typical of this strategy. Intermixed with music, messages, interviews, and fund-raising appeals, are invitations to become a Christian. One is encouraged to telephone to speak or pray with a bank of counselors standing by. Here it is not "walk forward" but "call in."

A fourth example is the popular Evangelism Explosion program developed by pastor James Kennedy at Coral Ridge Presbyterian Church in Florida. Church members are trained to go out two-by-two knocking on doors in their community. The conversation focuses on the question: "If you were to die tonight and stand before God, what would you say when he asked you, 'Why should I let you into my heaven'?" Hopefully, this leads to an opportunity to provide an answer based on one's trust and acceptance of the atoning work of Jesus Christ.

Finally, the social scientific approach of the "church growth" movement has stressed that successful evangelism normally proceeds within a given social milieu, rather than crossculturally. People are more likely to be converted if they do it in the context of their own racial, social and economic group where they feel comfortable. While this school is also interested in promoting better crosscultural mission, the usual paradigm for conversion becomes "believing in Jesus around people I feel comfortable with."

Any armchair criticism of these or other evangelistic movements, of course, is pretty cheap and shabby if the critic is doing nothing. There is something very valid going on in each approach: in any event, taking the message of Christ into the heart of the university in a systematic way, preaching to great crowds and calling for decision, reaching out to television's vast audience, knocking on neighbors' doors and showing concern for the afterlife, and stressing that evangelism begins in one's own circle of contacts. All of this is good. At the same time, however, how do these (or any other approaches) stack up against the New Testament? Are we employing biblical means? Are we seeking biblical ends?[1]

As Peter himself said, "It is time for judgment to begin with the family of God" (1 Pet 4:17). Self-criticism is not pleasant, and it is easily evaded when a crowd of admirers keeps reassuring us that we are a "success." In our own era, however, it is precisely this notion of "success" which ought to be held up to scrutiny. As Jacques Ellul and other social critics have pointed out, our culture idolizes success, defined as the fastest, most efficient achievement of measurable, quantifiable growth.[2] One distortion arises in promoting faith in Christ as the best means to the ends we desire on other grounds. The popular practice of promoting the testimonies of successful businessmen, star athletes and other celebrities as "models" of what conversion to Christ can do for you is worse than misguided; it represents a quasi-idolatrous association of wealth, power and personal glory with the gospel. It is true that some converts have become wealthier or more successful in their professions as a consequence of greater integrity, a commitment to performing quality work and the giving up of wasteful or destructive patterns of life. But at least as often, biblically and historically, conversion to Christ has meant the opposite: loss of position and reputation, suffering and poverty. The latter, of course, has no more intrinsic value than the former. The validity of the call to Christian conversion lies elsewhere than in either the success or the suffering which follows.

The strategies employed to win converts must be designed with great care. Christians, like the rest of their contemporaries, often act as though the (measurable) end justifies the means—almost any means. If the statistics show more church members, then "how they got there" is beside the point, so it seems. Success and efficient methods become self-justifying. Biblically, however, faithfulness and truth stand taller than success and efficiency. Unfaithfulness or untruth is never justified by "good" results. Part of the reason for this is that the results are affected and shaped, however subtly, by the means employed. If you succeed in frightening someone into a conversion based solely on the terrors of hell, the result is a convert for whom Christianity means "fire insurance." This is negative, self-centered, otherworldly, sub-biblical.

Understood correctly, of course, efficient strategizing does have a biblical place. Inefficiency and waste are no virtues. Paul will "become all things to all people" in order to save some. The point is that efficiency and success must always be radically subordinated to faithfulness and truth. What appears to be an unsuccessful act of faith (the cross, for example) will in God's end be a true success (the resurrection). We may or may not be able to detect this level of success, given our limited life and perspective. There is no doubt, of course, that God often brings good out of our mistakes. People for whom Jesus Christ means "fire insurance" or growth in next year's business often mature and grow beyond these initial, inadequate concepts, though this does not justify defective evangelistic practices. We should not allow this sort of realistic assessment of our imperfection to deter us from trying to win converts! But at the same time, we must reach for a better understanding of what evangelism is all about.

Intimately related to evangelism is apologetics, the giving of reasons for the truth of our proclamation. Just as there are many contemporary approaches to evangelism, so, too, a wide variety of apologetical systems compete for our attention and allegiance. The favorite biblical text used to justify this apologetical work is the quotation from Peter's first letter which heads this chapter. Unquestionably, Peter's counsel is important. It may well be true that *most* of us are inadequately prepared to give people reasons for our faith and hope in Christ. We may not realize this, of course, if we never talk to others about Jesus and thus avoid all questioning.

On the other hand, one suspects Peter might be surprised to discover what mountains of material have been produced, allegedly in compliance with his inspired counsel! From Paul in Athens (Acts 17) to Thomas Aquinas's development of the classical proofs of God's existence to Francis Schaeffer's cultural apologetics in our own generation, there is a long, well-developed tradition of arguing *for* the truth of Christianity and *against* its rivals. "Arguing people into the kingdom" might even be considered an alternative approach to evangelism (recall the five examples given above). C. S. Lewis reported that he was "dragged kicking and screaming into the kingdom of heaven by the sheer weight of the evidence." John Warwick Montgomery, a contemporary apologist, has borrowed Lewis's phrase to describe his own conversion.[3]

It is essential to develop a Christian mind and world view with deep and strong roots. When someone probes beneath the surface of our proclamation of the good news, they ought to discover a robust, thoughtful foundation. It is not enough to respond to our questioners with a sweet smile and a "just because." Nevertheless, when carefully examined, the assistance of contemporary apologists is sometimes of dubious value.

Part of the problem of modern apologetics is that some of it is characterized by sloppy, inadequate research. As science, philosophy or history it is sometimes pitiful and laden with errors of fact and interpretation. Many charges laid at the door of Søren Kierkegaard in Christian critiques of existentialism, for example, are pathetically ignorant of Kierkegaard's complex and brilliant thought. A popular Christian critique of the "fall of the Roman Empire," to take another example, shows incredible ignorance not only of the history of the period but of Augustine's own monumental fifth-century work on the subject in the *City of God*. Such examples could be multiplied. When these arguments are summarily rejected by our contemporaries, this is *not* the "suffering for Christ" or "suffering for doing right" of which Peter speaks! This is not the offense and the scandal of the cross. It is the offense of sloppy, scandalous scholarship. It begins with a laudable eagerness to advance the cause of Christ, but it is often sidetracked by premature, uncritical acclaim from devotees and enthusiasts in Christian retreat centers and churches. Of course, not all apologetic writers come under this indictment, but we should *beware* of these possible weaknesses.

A second problem of much contemporary apologetics has to do with the issues and questions which are chosen for energetic dispute. As discussed earlier, it is entirely appropriate to respond to the questions being raised by the world (chapter three). In other words, God invites us to bring our questions to him. Still, these questions represent our human agenda which is not necessarily identical to God's agenda. An apologetic effort which is wholly consumed with various human problems and objections may be, in the long run, a means of assisting people in *evading* the truly critical questions God wishes to raise. It is at least questionable, perhaps even demonic, that so much attention is given to the *beginning* (arguments about the "how" of creation) and the *end* (arguments about the exact calendar of future prophecies), both to the neglect of the center, Jesus Christ. So, too, vast energy is spent on arguments over the *form* (of biblical revelation, of apologetic logic and so on) to the neglect of the *substance* (what is God saying and doing). In all of this apologists may be yet a step further from reality in that they are often responding to these questions as they were put in earlier generations, rather than our own. It is not, then, just a matter of preoccupation with secondary issues, but *secondary issues from an earlier apologetic fight in bygone generations* that is drawing all this interest.[4] At this point, the apologist is mainly arguing with other apologists in a kind of antiquarian society having little to do with *either* the heart and core of Christian faith *or* the pressing questions and challenges of our era.

Finally, apologetics (like evangelism) must be criticized in terms of its methods. Too often, Christian apologists have tried to fight fire with fire. In response to a deadening rationalism, some apologists become superrationalists, articulating a rationalistic (per)version of the faith. In response to a reductionistic scientific naturalism, some writers present voluminous "scientific proofs" that, for example, men have survived in the stomachs of whales (thus Jonah is believable), that the plagues of Egypt are scientifically explicable and so on. The arrogance of science and critical philosophy needs to be challenged—in careful, well-researched counter-arguments. But we must beware the subtle seduction of the enemy's means and methods.

At its worst, apologetics can turn into sub-Christian negativism and sarcasm. If, in a public debate with an opponent, the Christian apologist displays vastly superior erudition and scholarship, well and good. If he then insults and derides this opponent publicly, everything is undone. The meek, not the acidic and arrogant, shall inherit the earth! Peter says, "be prepared to give an answer . . . but *do this with gentleness and respect*" (1 Pet 3:15-16). An evil, malicious means will undermine the best intentions and truest message.

The solution to these problems is not to abandon the apologetic task and replace it with a blank stare! It is rather to return to the New Testament and recapture its spirit and style.

The Spirit-filled Evangelist and Apologist (Acts 2)

Everything began with the miracle of God's intervention. On the day of Pentecost God contradicted the natural, fallen order by enabling the disciples to speak in foreign languages. Members of many different foreign countries in Jerusalem that day were astonished to hear God's good news in their own languages. The miracle was an exact reversal of the story of the tower of Babel in the Old Testament, where confusion of languages drove people away from each other (Gen 11:1-9). The Pentecost miracle consisted of being addressed personally in one's own language and being drawn together, by God's Spirit and Word, with people from whom one was normally alienated.

To the miracle of Pentecost some people responded with sincere curiosity ("What is going on here? How can these people be doing this?") and others with derision ("This is crazy! You must be drunk!"). Peter's opening move as he stood up was to explain the miracle. "I hear some of you out there saying we're drunk! But that's impossible: it's only nine o'clock in the morning!"[5] What is happening here, Peter went on to explain, is exactly what the prophet Joel predicted (Joel 2:28-32): God is pouring out his Spirit and making this miraculous event possible. It is God who deserves all the credit for this, not us. Anyone who calls on the name of the Lord will be saved.

The miracle occurred. The people gathered. Peter explained the miracle, giving God all the credit and invited them to call on the Lord. His explanation was rooted directly in one of the prophets his audience recognized (correctly) as being a true messenger of God (Acts 2:1-21).

Peter then moved to the heart of his message: Jesus Christ (vv. 22-36). (1) Jesus was a man from Nazareth with an extraordinary life, accredited by God through his marvelous works. (2) Jesus was put to death by crucifixion—through the hands of wicked men—but nevertheless in accordance with God's purposes. (3) Jesus was raised by God from the dead—death and the grave could not hold him. David, our forefather, predicted this (Ps 16) and we ourselves stand here as witnesses to the resurrection. (4) Jesus is now ascended and exalted at the right hand of God—again, as David predicted (Ps 110). (5) It is Jesus who has poured out his Spirit on his followers, as you can see for yourselves. (6) Thus, this crucified Jesus is now true Lord and Messiah.

It was precisely this clear, straightforward presentation of Jesus Christ that "cut to the heart" of the audience (v. 37). People called out, "What shall we do?" Peter concluded with a hope-filled call for a no and a yes, like that he had heard from Jesus at his own conversion. "Repent" of your sins; say "No" to your past life of rejecting God and living for yourself. "Be baptized" as a great "Yes" to identification with Jesus Christ. You will be forgiven and you will receive God's Holy Spirit. This promise is not just for you but for all of your children and for anyone who calls on the name of the Lord. Peter continued to urge, "Save yourselves from this corrupt generation."

Peter did not pedal "cheap grace," that is, grace without repentance and discipleship. He called a spade a spade, forcing them to face up to the sin that separated them from God—and then offered them great hope in Jesus Christ. Everything turned on who Jesus Christ was, and on their relationship to this person. Peter did not preach the church, though it was the miracle of the Spirit in the church that provoked everything. He preached the "gospel of the kingdom," which was nothing less than the gospel of the King, Jesus Christ, the word of eternal life available through repentance and faith. As a result of Peter's message, the crowd's question changed from "What's going on here?" to "What shall *we* do?"—general curiosity turned to personal conviction.

Peter's second sermon followed a similar pattern (Acts 3). A cripple begging at the temple gate was miraculously healed. An astounded crowd gathered. Peter deflected all credit for the healing and insisted that it was the power of God, in combination with the man's faith in Jesus, that made him whole (Acts 3:12, 16). The center of Peter's message was the person of Jesus Christ: God raised up his servant Jesus and sent him to the people to bless them and turn them from evil. Jesus was denied and delivered to Pilate for execution. God raised him from the dead. He is now glorified in heaven but will come again. Moses and all the prophets bore witness to this Jesus, and we are standing here as witnesses to him and his resurrection. You must repent and turn to Jesus Christ, who promises forgiveness and "times of refreshing" in his presence.

Rudely arrested and jailed at the end of this message, Peter's third message was a brief statement to the "rulers and elders" (Acts 4:8-19). The event (the healing of the cripple) was, frankly, undeniable. The boldness and conviction of Peter also amazed the council. Responding to questioning, Peter stressed that the healing was the work of Jesus of Nazareth, the man they crucified, but whom God raised from the dead. As David alluded in the Psalms, the "stone rejected by the builders" is now the head cornerstone in God's building. Despite all warnings, Peter insisted, he must continue to speak about these things he had seen and heard. It was God's command.

In similar circumstances, Peter's fourth message was again addressed to the council (Acts 5:29-32). Jesus was killed. God raised him and exalted him to his right hand as Leader and Savior. Jesus offers repentance, forgiveness of sins and the gift of the Holy Spirit to those who obey him. Peter himself stood as a witness to this great news of Jesus Christ. Again, he affirmed that he must "obey God rather than men."

The fifth, and final, sermon of Peter recorded in Acts was that given to the gentile household of the military leader Cornelius (Acts 10:34-43). What led to this message was a vision or dream Cornelius had, urging him to invite Peter to speak to his household. Cornelius was already "god-fearing" and a searcher. God intervened in his life by urging him to contact Peter. Peter's message to this non-Jewish audience stressed God's impartiality and the universal scope of his salvation. Peter presented the details about the life of Jesus of Nazareth, his good deeds, healing, and the evident presence of God with him. But, Peter continued, he was crucified before being raised from the dead by God. He is ordained by God as the judge of the living and dead, but those who believe in him have forgiveness of their sins. Peter stressed the fact that he and the other disciples were eyewitnesses of Jesus' life, death and resurrection, but he mentioned that all of this is rooted also in the witness of the ancient prophets of Israel.

There is a certain variety evident in our five "evangelism and apologetics" episodes with Peter in Acts: addressing Jews (people with at least some, if not a great deal of, familiarity and respect for the Hebrew Bible) and (once) Gentiles; addressing internationals as well as local people; political and religious leaders as well as ordinary people; an inquisitive crowd of thousands, a few governmental tormentors and a household of Romans eager to listen. Still, we don't exactly have an example of one-on-one neighbor-to-neighbor evangelism—and we can easily think of other circumstances that might be rather different from Peter's experience (Philip, Priscilla, Paul, Stephen and other figures in Acts supply some other models, of course).

The question, however, is what we *can* learn from Peter's experiences. What light does this story shed on our evangelistic and apologetic patterns? The most obvious point is that in every situation, all attention is focused on Jesus Christ. Peter does not spend time promoting or analyzing "speaking in tongues," the exemplary love of Christians or reforms in local laws limiting religious freedom. He promotes the person of Jesus Christ. He gives credit to Jesus Christ for the health of a formerly ill person, or anything else that attracts peoples' awestruck attention. He tells who the person of Jesus was and is—details about his life, death, resurrection, ascension, future as well as current plans, and how one can know him.

Just as his own conversion was provoked by and centered on the person of Jesus Christ, Peter's evangelism leaves no doubt about the absolute centrality of Jesus. He calls people to a relationship of faith and trust in this person. The good news was about the kingdom of

God—all the way to the end of Acts with Paul preaching it in Rome
(Acts 28:31). In Acts as well as the Gospels, this meant proclaiming the
King, the gracious rule of Jesus Christ as Lord of those who would
follow him. What is new and different in Peter's preaching in Acts is
the depth and breadth of his view of Jesus. The story of the life of
Jesus of Nazareth by no means disappears, but Peter now stresses the
centrality of the cross, the resurrection and the glorification of his
Lord. The core remains the same: know and follow Jesus. The perspective on Jesus' meaning and importance is greatly enlarged.

Second, Peter "does apologetics" in each message; that is, he provides reasons for his proclamation of Jesus. But there is no apologetics separate from evangelism! His apologetic arguments are intimately
related to, and in service of, his proclamation of the good news of
Jesus. "Winning apologetic debates" has no independent importance
for Peter (or the New Testament). But planting, nourishing and pro-
tecting the seeds of new spiritual life have great importance. The
implications for the way we conceive and practice apologetics are
obvious.

Third, Peter's proclamation is closely associated with a preceding
or accompanying event in which God is at work. The communication
miracle of Pentecost, the healing of a crippled man, the swelling
interest in Christ, or the vision given to Cornelius—these events lead
to opportunities, invitations and even administrative orders to talk
about Jesus and what is happening. We must be careful not to deduce
an absolute rule here, such as, "Never speak until a clear action of
God has occurred." (There are examples of Jesus and others provoking the event by *first* announcing the Word of God.) But Peter's experience does suggest that a good deal, at least, of our evangelism may
most appropriately take place in this kind of context where God has
acted in the lives of others and ourselves—and some explanation is
called for. In Peter's own conversion experience, it was the miraculous
intervention of Jesus in his daily existence, his fishing business, that
provoked everything. God initiates the encounter with himself; his
action puts our normal existence—"business as usual"—in question.
When God is present in our daily existence among neighbors and
coworkers, we will often have our best opportunities for evangelism.

The *practice* of the presence of God may be followed by an effective *declaration* of the Word of God. If we *display* the love and care of our Lord, we may *speak* more persuasively about that Lord.

Fourth, the preceding or accompanying demonstration of God's presence not only provokes and sets the context for the proclamation, it is also one of three basic forms of apologetics employed by Peter. It stands as supporting evidence (not just an intriguing introduction) for the good news. The spectacular events of Pentecost and of the healing at the temple gate were evidence of God's reality. In our twentieth-century technological society, God's intervention will be just as profound, just as miraculous, as those we read about in the New Testament—though it will be so in relation to our cultural and historical situation, not that of first-century Palestine!

The spectacular sights and sounds of Pentecost, the successful command to a crippled man to "get up and walk"—these were important manifestations of God's power that "got the job done" in Peter's context. But it will be no less the action of God, and no less a preparation and apologetic for the gospel today, when Christians overcome the busy-ness and alienation of modern life to clearly, caringly, reach out to communicate the good news to people in their own language and daily existence. It will be no less important to use "ordinary" means to engage in extraordinarily loving actions to help heal a hurting person whose path crosses ours. Do these things and people will have ears to hear what you have to say.

More than any other "event," the demonstration of genuine love among Christian brothers and sisters (who would ordinarily be strangers to each other) serves as the ultimate preparation and apologetic for the proclamation of Jesus. As Jesus said to Peter and the disciples in his "farewell address," "by this all men will know that you are my disciples, if you love one another" (Jn 13:35). Jesus prayed "that all of them may be one, . . . so that the world may believe that you have sent me" (Jn 17:21). On the day of Pentecost the crowd saw a band of disciples that had been brought into "one accord." They heard a message which drew together people in Jerusalem from "every nation under heaven" (Acts 2:5). In the aftermath, people could observe that "all the believers were together and had everything in common" (Acts 2:44). Little wonder that "the Lord added to their number daily" (Acts 2:47).

Peter stressed all of this in his first letter. Do not be shaped by your old ignorant life, he writes, but be holy, like God, in everything you do (1 Pet 1:14-15). Above all, "love one another deeply, from the heart" (1:22; 4:8). "Live such good lives among the pagans that, though they accuse you of doing wrong, they may see your good deeds and glorify God" (2:12). "It is God's will that by doing good you should silence the ignorant talk of foolish men" (2:15). Wives of unbelieving husbands can "win over" these men by their behavior, doing what is right without fear (3:1-6). Behavior that is transformed by God's love, life that exhibits God's definition of the "good" and the "right," is the *primary* apologetic Peter advocates in his letter.

The full text of Peter's well-known "call to apologetics" is worth careful attention:

> In your hearts set apart Christ as Lord. Always be prepared to give an answer to everyone who asks you to give the reason for the hope that you have. But do this with gentleness and respect, keeping a clear conscience, so that those who speak maliciously against your good behavior in Christ may be ashamed of their slander. (1 Pet 3:15-16)

Far from a retreat to silence, Peter urges Christian disciples to "declare the praises" of Jesus Christ (2:9) and "give an answer" to their questioners (3:15). This should be done with boldness and freedom, but also with "gentleness and respect." Even in the great apologetics text cited above, there is a close association between the "good answer" and "good behavior." The clear implication is that our apologetics is, or ought often to be, in response to questions raised by our "hope" and our "good behavior"—not necessarily by some powerful, philosophical argument we have promulgated.[6]

Nonetheless, the "event" is only one of three types of evidence mustered by Peter in support of his introduction of Jesus Christ. Peter also, in all five messages, stresses that he (and the other disciples) are *eyewitnesses* to the truth about Jesus Christ. In particular, the resurrection of Jesus Christ is a great fact to which they can attest. In his second letter, Peter reminded the recipients about the truth of Christianity (illustrated in this instance by the transfiguration episode):

> We did not follow cleverly invented stories when we told you about
> the power and coming of our Lord Jesus Christ, but we were eye-
> witnesses of his majesty. For he received honor and glory from God
> the Father when the voice came to him from the Majestic Glory,
> saying, "This is my Son, whom I love; with him I am well pleased."
> We ourselves heard this voice that came from heaven when we
> were with him on the sacred mountain. (2 Pet 1:16-18)

Peter's claim to be an eyewitness was an implicit invitation to examine
his testimony and its credibility. While we do not have the living Peter
with us for our examination, we do have his testimony (and that of
other early witnesses), which can be read and weighed like other
historical materials.

There is no such thing as an airtight, logically compelling historical
proof that Jesus was, in fact, "transfigured" on the mountain, or that
he literally rose from the dead. History weighs all the evidence and
develops more or less "probable" reconstructions and explanations of
past events—including "natural" events, as well as the singular,
unique, even "supernatural" events of history. *Much* of our knowledge
of the ancient world is based on evidence given by only one dubious
source or another. But this does not prevent historians from making
historical judgments and reconstructing events.

Provided that one does not *presuppose* the impossibility of the existence of God and the possibility of the incarnation of God in Jesus
Christ (no easy task for those propagandized by a narrow-minded,
reductionist, scientific naturalism), the best historical explanation for
the beginnings of Christianity is that Jesus was, in fact, God incarnate,
and that his life, death and resurrection were as reported in the New
Testament documents. It is the most sensible explanation for the
amazing rise and spread of Christianity and for the transformation of
a small, beleaguered band of followers into a courageous movement
willing to endure incredible hardship, suffering and even death.

If Jesus was not who he said he was, if he did not rise from the dead,
we must summon up an awesome credulity and believe that this remarkable community was based on either a *lie* (the disciples constantly stressed that Satan was the very "father of lies" and truth was a

central virtue) or an ignorant, misguided *myth* (all of their teaching
and behavior reflects thoughtful, intelligent, careful minds at work).
None of this is an irresistible "truth"—many intelligent critics resist
acceptance of this historical explanation. Nor does acceptance of a set
of historical conclusions about the identity of Jesus as Savior, Lord
and God, by itself, make one a Christian. The latter occurs only when
a person enters into personal, living relationship with Jesus as Lord.
Nevertheless, the historical eyewitness accounts present a valuable
part of the "answer" for those who wish to know why we follow Jesus
Christ.[7]

The third form of Peter's apologetics consisted in showing how
Jesus was not an isolated phenomenon but was the culmination of a
long tradition of biblical prophecy. In his speeches to Jewish audiences Peter freely quoted from the writings of Moses, David and Joel, to
show how Jesus fulfilled the expectations of these early spokesmen
for God. But even to Cornelius (a Gentile who could not be expected
to know or accept the authority of Israel's prophets), Peter alluded to
the witness of "all the prophets." In his second letter, Peter summa-
rized his position as follows:

> We have the word of the prophets made more certain, and you will
> do well to pay attention to it, as to a light shining in a dark place,
> until the day dawns and the morning star rises in your hearts.
> Above all, you must understand that no prophecy of Scripture came
> about by the prophet's own interpretation. For prophecy never had
> its origin in the will of man, but men spoke from God as they were
> carried along by the Holy Spirit. (2 Pet 1:19-21)

So, too, Peter's first letter is filled with references to past prophecies
which predict and illuminate the meaning of the sufferings as well as
the glory of Jesus Christ (see 1:10-12). Peter quotes from (or alludes
to) Genesis, Leviticus, Isaiah (especially the "suffering servant" and
"cornerstone" passages in Is 8, 28 and 53), Psalms, Proverbs and
Hosea. His second letter uses some of these same prophetic texts and
others as well.

Clearly, for a Jewish audience that held the Old Testament in great
respect as the Word of God, such citations of the prophets would have
particular power. But even for those (like Cornelius) who did not

approach Jesus Christ with this background, the role of Scripture is important. This is so partly because of the remarkable *predictive* character of ancient prophecy. It is indisputable that Israel had a deep-rooted, multifaceted "messianic expectation." Jesus' correspondence with this complex picture (which becomes unified and meaningful, above all, if he is regarded as the fulfillment) is extraordinary and impressive. Still, Peter's appeal to Scripture has a significance broader than a mere identification of specific predictions which came true in Jesus. For Peter, the whole of Scripture (and in 2 Pet 3:16 he even refers to Paul's writings as part of Holy Scripture!) is the Christ-centered texture of the faith. The Bible gives a wholeness, richness and depth to the events and teachings of Jesus. The Scripture enlarges and fills out a Christocentric view of what is happening in human history. The unity of all these diverse writings is precisely in the person of Jesus Christ.

This example of Peter's apologetic method should encourage us to become deeply familiar with the content and movement of Scripture. When questioned about the hope that we have in Christ, we should be prepared to share the deeper, broader dimensions of this biblical world view centered on Jesus Christ.[8] Jesus is best appreciated when seen in the full context of creation, Fall, exodus, covenant, exile and eschaton. These things do not have independent or formal interest for Peter, however: their meaning turns on the person of Jesus Christ. The Christian hope is not, for example, a utopian return to some golden age of unspoiled "orders of creation," but rather God's future kingdom which has now broken into our history in the living, dying, rising Jesus of Nazareth.

To review again: the event occurred. Peter explained it and then focused all attention on the person of Christ. In support of his message he provided not only the fact of the "event" but the evidence of eyewitness accounts and ancient prophecy. The *final* aspect of his message, then, was a clear call to decision, involving both the "No" and the "Yes." That is, he asserted the responsibility and accountability of his listeners before God. They must repent of their sinfulness, say no to the self in its rebellion against God. But they must also say yes to God by faith in Jesus Christ. This is God's gracious offer of salvation to the lost, forgiveness for the offenders. It is a great hope and a promise not only for the future but for "times of refreshing" by the presence of God's Spirit now.

Peter urged baptism as a vivid symbol of this conversion to Jesus Christ. It is not enough to say a few words or have a good attitude. Repentance and faith must be clear-cut and demonstrated by action. Baptism is not a *work* to earn this salvation, but an *act* to symbolize one's public identification with the work of Jesus Christ in dying and rising again. It symbolizes both to oneself and to the world the decision to leave all and follow Jesus Christ. "This water symbolizes baptism that now saves you also—not the removal of dirt from the body but the pledge of a good conscience toward God. It saves you by the resurrection of Jesus Christ" (1 Pet 3:21). Baptism is a symbol whose meaning derives from the resurrection of Jesus Christ.

The Reaction (Acts 2:41-47)

The call is to be faithful—to do what is right, whether it is observably effective or not. The reactions to Peter's messages displayed the usual range we may expect in all generations. There were some who radically and decisively rejected what he had to say: some rulers responded with beatings, jail and threats. Others, notably an honored teacher of the law named Gamaliel, held off a decision for further observation and reflection (see Acts 5:34-40). In neither case did Peter leave with his head down, viewing his evangelism and apologetics as a failure. To the contrary he rejoiced, even when he suffered personally, for the good news had been proclaimed in faithfulness and courage. Like his Lord, he had taken a few blows for speaking the truth.

However, in other cases the response was an enthusiastic acceptance of the gospel. The description in Acts 2 is a model of the results that we ought to hope and pray for. The priorities are quite clear: first and always, we must be *faithful* in continually bearing accurate, biblical witness to Jesus Christ. Second, we would like to be *effective* in persuading as many people as possible to begin lives of discipleship under the lordship of Jesus Christ. These priorities must never be lost—or reversed.

The worst results of our proclamation are when our listeners turn away with a bored, apathetic yawn *or* with hostility, generated not by the cross of Jesus Christ but by our offensiveness, arrogance, ignorance or hypocrisy. If our listeners respond with rejection of Jesus Christ (and of us as faithful representatives), fine; that is to be expected on occasion. It is not easy to face up to reality and be called to repent before the crucified, resurrected Jesus. If our listeners react by wishing more time to observe and investigate (like Gamaliel), this is also to be expected and ought to be met in return by patience and hope on our part (consider Jesus' and Andrew's patience after Peter's first encounter). This is not the same thing as boredom and apathy. The seed has been planted; be patient for the harvest.

What we most deeply desire as an effect of our evangelism and apologetics, however, is the "model response" to Peter's message in Acts 2:41-47. About three thousand listeners (1) received the word, (2) were baptized and added to the community of faith. These people then devoted themselves to (3) the apostles' teaching, (4) the fellowship, (5) the breaking of bread and (6) prayer. All of the believers (7) treated their possessions as a common heritage and shared with anyone who had need. In daily life they (8) met together, eating and breaking bread with "glad and sincere hearts." They (9) "praised God" and (10) "enjoyed the favor of all the people," more of whom were saved day by day.

This was clearly a church built on "the Rock," in all the senses discussed earlier (chapter four). It was built on Jesus Christ, the chief cornerstone, the dominant theme of the message to which the people responded. It was built on the foundation of the apostles and prophets. It was built of ordinary people who, in turn, became "living stones" through the faithful proclamation of Peter.

These were authentic conversions in that they consisted of entering into personal relationship with Jesus Christ. At the decisive point of conversion, both repentance and faith (the no and the yes) are demonstrated not only in word but in deed (beginning with the powerful symbol of baptism). With conversion the threefold life task of discipleship commences. A vibrant community of brothers and sisters with, and for, Jesus Christ takes shape. This community is simultaneously a place of worship (breaking bread, prayers, praising God), a place of learning (the apostles' teaching) and caring (sharing daily life, eating together, economic sharing with those in need). Their presence in the city constituted a powerful outward witness, in response to which more and more people came to know Christ as Savior and Lord.

Evangelism and apologetics are neither a business nor a game. They are the activity of the grace and truth of God's Word bringing life to a needy world through our lips. Peter is not the only evangelist or apologist deserving our study, but he does represent one basic New Testament paradigm or model of the truly charismatic (Spirit-filled) proclaimer of the gospel. So, too, his converts are not the only ones we can learn from in the New Testament, but their portrayal in Acts is a very important contribution to our understanding of the evange-listic/apologetic results we seek. Beginning with ourselves and our own church, a great deal can be gained by self-criticism and reform aided by these inspired models.

For Reflection or Discussion

1. Have you ever been asked to "give reasons" for your faith in Jesus Christ? What did you say? How did the person respond to your answers?

2. What, specifically and concretely, can be done in your own life, and in the activities of your home church, to prepare and mobilize more faithful and effective evangelism and apologetics?

3. Peter and the disciples followed Jesus' strategy of beginning in Jerusalem, then Judea, then moving out to neighboring Samaria, and eventually reach-ing out to the ends of the earth (Acts 1:8). Where can you begin? What strategy can you outline for expanding your proclamation and outreach?

10 Battling the Powers: Sharing, Liberating and Healing

"Jesus Christ . . . has gone into heaven
and is at God's right hand—with angels,
authorities and powers in submission to him."

PETER'S CAREER AS AN APOSTLE IN THE BOOK OF ACTS CARRIES FORWARD
the same three tasks of discipleship which he began while following
in the (literal) footsteps of Jesus of Nazareth. He cultivates the relationship with God personally and in the new community (see chapter
eight). He engages in vigorous proclamation of God's Word (see chapter nine). He carries on the program of healing and exorcism. In the
present chapter we will review his three-dimensional conflict with the
"principalities and powers" reported in the first half of the book of
Acts.

Part of Christian growth in discipleship involves a thoughtful adop-
tion of the world view and philosophy of history revealed in Scripture
and centered on Jesus Christ. "Like newborn babies, crave pure spiritual milk, so that by it you may grow up in your salvation, now that
you have tasted that the Lord is good" (1 Pet 2:2-3). It does not take
much reading of the Bible to discover a world influenced not only by
a supernatural God with his Holy Spirit and hosts of angels but also

by Satan, a devil, an enemy prowling "around like a roaring lion looking for someone to devour" (1 Pet 5:8). Often in the service of this enemy are various "principalities and powers," demonic forces waging war against God and his creation. Peter calls us to resist this enemy. In similar fashion, Paul calls Christians to wrestle, to fight back, in this spiritual warfare (see Eph 6:10-20).

It has not always been easy for twentieth-century men and women to understand or accept this biblical cosmology. The methods of science and technology, which work well in their own domain, have been notably unproductive as avenues toward understanding many other aspects of human life. Wisdom, meaning and happiness are just three components of human life unreachable by science and technology. Also, with respect to anything supernatural, transcendent, unique or broadly transhistorical, methods refined in laboratories are pathetically myopic and even blind. Unfortunately, much of our civilization has bowed down in abject worship of these methods. It requires a resolute will to be open-minded in order to overcome such brainwashing.

Still, one must not too quickly assume that modern, scientific human beings are uniformly predisposed against all of the supernatural. On the one hand, the most vigorous growth of Satanism, soothsayers, fortunetellers, mysticism and the occult is precisely in Paris, Berkeley and other bastions of modern learning! On the other hand, many Christian churches are flooded by highly trained scientists, technicians and intellectuals who have no difficulty in affirming the miraculous. In short, the milieu in which we seek to recover a fully biblical world view is characterized by a high degree of chaos and contradiction, resistance and openness.

It is difficult enough to figure out what the biblical writers themselves were trying to convey in their demonic or apocalyptic imagery! But this difficulty is compounded for us by centuries of medieval (and modern) art and literature which have provided us with vivid (but perhaps misleading) interpretations of the biblical imagery. We have to penetrate behind images of images to arrive at the truth.

But Christians ought to explore this biblical cosmology with its principalities and powers, first of all, because Jesus Christ, the prophets and the apostles consider it true and important. It is part of the Word of God. But this world view also makes sense of the world as we experience it. The shoe fits, and we do well to put it on. In brief outline, we may note the following from Scripture: (1) God is Creator, Redeemer, and Lord of all—absolutely good and ultimately in control of all that is. (2) Nevertheless, within the freedom given by God, powers of evil are *real* in our universe—and are not merely ignorance or the absence of good but have their own "weight" and force. (3) This evil manifests itself in individual perversity but is also supraindividual, suprahistorical and supernatural, invading and deforming structures and institutions as much as individuals. (4) Jesus Christ has disarmed, defeated and made a public example of the principalities and powers in his cross and resurrection (Col 2:15) and "has gone into heaven and is at God's right hand—with angels, authorities and powers in submission to him" (1 Pet 3:22). (5) However, until the final judgment, the powers of evil continue to exercise a baleful influence on human history, especially when constituted or reinstated as such by human beings. (6) Thus, Christians are called to combat these powers and, with the power of the Holy Spirit, make present and real the victory of their Lord.[1]

In Peter's case there were three fronts on which this battle took place: politics, economics and health. The power of evil is not, of course, limited to these three domains! There is reason, however, to view these three as primary battlefields. The temptation of Jesus in the wilderness, for example, had a political dimension ("the kingdoms of the world"), an economic dimension ("command these stones to be made bread") and a health dimension ("flaunt death by throwing yourself off this height"; "create bread to appease your hunger"). Each of these factors was manipulated by Satan against Jesus. In his death and resurrection, also, Jesus "made a public example" of the powers of death (the ultimate "health" problem), economics (betrayed for thirty pieces of silver) and politics (crucified by popular "vote" and by Jewish and Roman authorities). He exposed these powers in their evil reality; his resurrection won the victory over each of them.

In the most convincing interpretation of the famous apocalyptic imagery of Revelation, Jesus Christ (the Lamb who was slain) alone is able to open the seals of the scroll giving the true meaning of history. The seals unveil the primary components of history (Rev 6). The rider of the white horse represents the Word of God (see Rev 19:11-13), the first and ultimate factor in history. The rider of the red horse represents violence, and the sword, the power of the state. The rider of the black horse represents the economic power. The rider of the pale horse represents death by sword, famine and pestilence, the sources of virtually all health problems. The prayers and faithful witness of God's people are the fifth factor. The cataclysmic onset of the final day of the Lord is the sixth factor. Many other biblical texts could be cited, of course. In short, however, there is ample evidence that in the biblical world view a decisive combat is occurring between rebellious powers active in politics, economics and death, on the one hand, and the Word and action of God with the complicity of his faithful witnesses on the other.

The Fight against Mammon

As surprising as it may seem, Jesus had more to say to his disciples about the evil potential of money, property and wealth than he did about heaven and hell! Most of us are familiar with his parables and teaching about the dangers of greed, acquisitiveness and anxiety over such things. He confronted the rich young ruler with a challenge to sell what he had and give to the poor. He warned of the great difficulty of the rich getting saved ("harder than a camel going through the eye of a needle"—but possible with God!). He sent out his disciples to live in simplicity. In his most decisive contrast, Jesus said, "No one can serve two masters. You cannot serve God and mammon" (Mt 6:24 RSV).

Money (and property) becomes the idol "Mammon" when it receives the sacrifice of our life and energy. Pieces of metal and paper become the domain of the principalities and powers when they hold us in their grip as tightly as an absolute monarch ruling his subjects. Not just our relationship to God but our relationships to other people, to the earth and to our self are distorted by the worshipful addiction to money. The best test of whether we are in the grip of this power is to occasionally go "cold turkey": do without it or refuse it when we crave it. The best tactic to insure a desacralization of Mammon in our lives is to give it away regularly and even sacrificially.[2]

With its "power" unmasked, stripped of its idolatrous hold on us, money (and property) can once again function in the service of God and of life, as a humble, material means of no intrinsic value by itself. "Silver or gold I do not have," Peter said to the crippled man begging on the temple steps. "But what I have I give you. In the name of Jesus Christ of Nazareth, walk" (Acts 3:6). The gift of God was something much greater and more fundamental than money. No less significant, a few months or years later in Samaria, Simon the magician "begged" Peter to sell him the power to lay hands on people and convey the Holy Spirit. Peter's response was emphatic: "May your money perish with you, because you thought you could buy the gift of God with money!" (Acts 8:18-20). Despite many aberrations over the centuries (for example, the selling of indulgences, which aggravated Martin Luther), the truth of Christianity remains: God's gifts are much better and more fundamental than money; God's gifts cannot be purchased with money.

The combat with the power of money came to a head early in Peter's experience in Acts. One of the greatest revolutions in the lives of the early Christians (stressed both in Acts 2:44-46 and 4:32-37) was a radical transformation in their attitude and relationship toward money and property. No longer claiming anything as their own, they treated their money and property as a common heritage to be shared according to need. The root meaning of Christian *koinonia* or *fellowship* is really "community," a common, shared life, having an economic dimension. Luke says that "many wonders and miraculous signs were done by the apostles. All the believers were together and had everything in common. Selling their possessions and goods, they gave to anyone as [any] had need. . . . They . . . ate together with glad and sincere hearts" (Acts 2:43-46). Not least of these "signs and wonders" must have been the willingness to break the clutches of individual possessiveness and share with generous, glad hearts!

In Acts 4 Luke again reports this phenomenon:

All the believers were one heart and mind. No one claimed that any of his possessions was his own, but they shared everything they

had. With great power the apostles continued to testify to the resurrection of the Lord Jesus, and much grace was upon them all.
There were no needy persons among them. For from time to time
those who owned lands or houses sold them, brought the money
from the sales and put it at the apostles' feet, and it was distributed
to anyone as [any] had need. (Acts 4:32-35)

There was not a needy person among them. "Great grace" was upon
them all. "Great power" was manifested in their proclamation of the
gospel. Mammon had been toppled, with marvelous benefits to all.

Luke cites one specific individual, "Barnabas," later a noteworthy
companion of both Paul and Mark in their travels, as an example of
the new regime: he sold a field which belonged to him and contributed the proceeds to the community. Unfortunately a husband and
wife, Ananias and Sapphira, also sold a field and came publicly do-
nating their gift to the community of Christ. Except they lied about
it, and quietly kept a chunk of the proceeds for themselves. When
confronted by Peter about the seriousness of this lie to the Holy Spirit,
both Ananias and Sapphira dropped dead on the spot. The problem
was *not* that they had violated a mandatory rule to sell everything. As
Peter said to Ananias, "Didn't it belong to you before it was sold? And
after it was sold, wasn't the money at your disposal?" The problem was
the lie and the hypocrisy of pretending to donate all, while keeping
a part. Ananias and Sapphira lost the battle against Mammon. They
died as victims of the power of money.

Just as in other New Testament stories we have been studying, we
must hold tightly and tenaciously to the principle revealed by God but
"sit loose" on the historical details peculiar to a given situation. Now,
as then, our spiritual combat will take place partly in a contest against
the demonic power of Mammon, against an idolatry of consumerism,
money, property, materialism. Whether we live on donations, salary,
commissions or welfare, whether we formally own property, rent,
lease or borrow, everything must be placed under the rule of Jesus
Christ our Lord. *Everything,* not just a tithe. Our primary purpose is
to "seek the kingdom of God and its righteousness"; all financial
matters must take a back seat in subordination to that life purpose.
When we do deal with money and property, we should regard it as

a humble, relative means of meeting people's needs—other people as well as ourselves and our own families. In meeting needs we should be generous and joyful, not grouchy, ostentatious or miserly. And while we have an inescapable individual stewardship to exercise, we should participate joyfully and generously in the common efforts of the community of faith. (The early contributors to the common fund did not, apparently, tie strings to their donations to the common fund!)

In his letters Peter reminds Christians that their true inheritance is with God in Jesus Christ. Their redemption is in the sacrifice of Christ, not "perishable things like silver and gold." Their faith is "of greater worth than gold, which perishes even though refined by fire" (1 Pet 1:4, 7, 18). Even teachers and church leaders must be on guard against the "way of Balaam," whose greed led him to "love the wages of wickedness" (2 Pet 2:3, 14-16). The true shepherd of God's flock must be a willing servant "not greedy for money, but eager to serve" (1 Pet 5:2).

A complete biblical theology of money requires the teaching of Jesus, Paul and all the rest of Scripture, of course. Peter's experiences, however, point us in the right direction and show us the basic outlines of this front in the continuing combat against one of the most insidious of the principalities and powers.

The Struggle against Babylon

Another formidable opponent against which Peter and Christian disciples must struggle is a political power transformed into demonic Babylon. The problem with the state occurs when its monopoly of force turns into an unjust display of violence against its own citizens as well as those beyond its borders. It also occurs when its call for citizen loyalty is transmuted into an idolatrous demand for total submission and even worship. At its worst the state becomes totalitarian and authoritarian (so with Caligula, Nero, Hitler, Khomeini). At its best the state can be a humble organization of certain aspects of the common life of its citizens. It can be a veritable "servant of God" in suppressing evil and promoting good (see Rom 13:1-7).[3]

In the company of Jesus, Peter learned that a disciple must "give to

God" only the things that are God's (that is, human beings who bear God's image), but that one ought also "give to Caesar" some things that are in his domain (such as taxes, money that "bears his image" and respect—Mk 12:16-17). He learned that his true, absolute citizenship was in the kingdom of God, even though he lived in a kingdom of the world. Through sad experience Peter was rebuked for taking up the violent sword of the world—even in the cause of defending his Lord. Babylon played a major role in nailing Jesus to the cross after a bogus legal trial. With the weapons of the Spirit which raised him from the dead, Jesus defeated this power, and commissioned his followers to walk in the same path no matter what the circumstances.

Peter's four encounters with political powers in Acts and his comments written while living in Rome during the end of his life give us some helpful perspective on our struggle to "exorcise" the demonic from the political arena. His first two encounters were with the Sanhedrin, the council of rabbis and representatives of the great families. That this was not merely a religious body is attested by the fact that they were able to jail and flog Peter and others. The lines between political and religious authority were not clearly drawn. The Sanhedrin included many Sadducees who were well known as collaborators with the occupying Roman Imperial regime. In Acts 4 Peter and his long-time associate John of Zebedee were summarily arrested and jailed overnight by the council, who were angered by their activity in healing the crippled man on the temple steps and even more so because of their proclamation of the resurrected Jesus.

At their hearing the next day, Peter and John were asked, "by what power or what name did you do this?" (Acts 4:7). Peter responded with a brief, clear message that it was in the name of Jesus Christ, whom they had crucified. "There is no other name under heaven given to men by which we must be saved" (Acts 4:12). The council conferred but decided that since the healing was indisputable, and masses of people were behind them in support, they would simply order them not to speak any more about Jesus. Peter's reply was, "Judge for yourselves whether it is right in God's sight to obey you rather than God. For we cannot help speaking about what we have seen and heard" (Acts 4:19-20).

Not long after this the Sanhedrin, again "filled with jealousy," arrested the apostles and put them in the common prison. In the middle of the night "an angel of the Lord opened the doors at the jail and brought them out" and urged them to continue their public teaching the next morning (Acts 5:17-20). The bewildered authorities the next day received news that their prisoners were out preaching to the people in the temple! "At that, the captain went with his officers and brought the apostles. They did not use force, because they feared that the people would stone them" (5:26). Questioned about this civil disobedience, Peter replied in his famous phrase, "We must obey God rather than men" (5:29). His listeners "were furious and wanted to put them to death," but Gamaliel, a wise old rabbi on the council (and one of Paul's teachers), urged a "wait and see" attitude which won their consent. Peter and his associates were then flogged and ordered again to stop preaching.

Whatever might be the legitimate business of the council, the line was crossed when it tried to usurp the place of God. The priorities were clear: God alone deserves absolute obedience, the human authorities have a lesser claim on Peter and the disciples. In the case of a conflict, God must be obeyed, even if this implied civil disobedience. Peter went to jail. He submitted nonviolently to a flogging. But he continued to obey God by preaching and healing. He accepted the miraculous "illegal" deliverance out of jail by the angel of the Lord. The ambitious power of the state was successfully contested by the power of God's Spirit.

Peter's third encounter with political authorities was of a radically different order. Several years after these first two skirmishes he was summoned once again by a political authority. This time, though, it was Cornelius (Acts 10). Not only was Cornelius a Gentile, he was a representative of the Roman imperial government. Not only was he a Roman, he was a military leader. Yet Cornelius was a seeker whose prayers were heard by God. Peter's message was again Jesus Christ, and a great conversion story unfolded.

The vast majority of Christians refused to participate in war and military service during the first two and a half hopeful centuries of the growth of Christianity. They were despised for this by critics of the faith, but they buckled to pressure to take up the weapons of the world only after the Emperor Constantine was converted in A.D. 312 and began the process of "Christianizing" the world (that is, "paganizing" the church). It is essential to note, in any case, that God was at work in the personnel of the state and the military, and that Peter did not begin by criticizing Cornelius's position or asking for his resignation. Peter simply brought together Jesus Christ and Cornelius. Having accomplished this, he allowed time and space for further growth in Cornelius's political and vocational discipleship. Concentration on the life-changing core of the gospel was followed by patiently awaiting growth and the implications of conversion and discipleship.

In the early forties Peter was shaken by the abrupt arrest and murder of James, his long-time friend and fishing partner. Herod Agrippa I, the grandson of Herod the Great and a loyal puppet of emperors Claudius and Caligula, had carried out this crime in an attempt to curry favor with the Jewish majority. Seeing that this constituency was pleased, Herod proceeded to jail Peter during the Passover season, intending the same fate for him. Amid extremely tight security, Peter was for the second time miraculously delivered from the jaws of death through the assistance of an angel of the Lord. Free outside the prison, Peter went to the home of Mary, the mother of Mark, where a large group of disciples had gathered for prayer. A girl named Rhoda answered his knocks on the gate but ran back inside (forgetting to unlock the gate) to report her "vision" of Peter. When she finally convinced others to come and see, Peter was let inside for a very happy, astonishing reunion. Peter then "left for another place" safely away from Herod's troops. Herod had the guards executed for allowing Peter to escape. Herod himself died in A.D. 44, struck down "by an angel of the Lord" when he yielded in self-delusion to the acclaim of the people that he was "the voice of a god, not of a man" (Acts 12:17-23).

As he was led away to await execution during Passover season, Peter's mind must have gone back a decade to the terrible events of Jesus' arrest and crucifixion. He had claimed then that he would follow his Lord to death, if necessary, but he had miserably failed. Jesus had warned him that one day he would face an involuntary

death. The hour had come it seemed. He was imprisoned, guarded
by four squadrons of soldiers (sixteen total). He was chained between
two soldiers, locked inside the prison. But the angel of the Lord
appeared, the chains fell off, the guards remained asleep and Peter
followed his deliverer past two sets of guards through the open gate
into the city. It was impossible. But with the God of resurrection, all
things become possible. Even the confusion over Peter's identity at the
gate of Mary's house bore an uncanny resemblance to the uncertainty
around some of the resurrection appearances of the Lord.

In this episode the conflict between Christ and Babylon took on
epic proportions. It was a conflict to the death. By setting Peter free,
the power of God defeated a demonic, death-dealing political power.
Just as the "angel of the Lord" was involved in the liberation, an
"angel of the Lord" struck down Herod in the moment of his supreme
arrogance and self-worship.

Twenty years after this miraculous escape, Peter wrote some further
political advice from the heart of Babylon (Rome). A persecution was
threatening on the horizon. Paul had already been arrested and await-
ed trial in Rome. Nero was exemplifying the worst kind of autocratic
repression. Fundamentally, Peter argued that Christians are members
of another "holy nation, a people belonging to God. . . . Once you
were not a people, but now you are the people of God" (1 Pet 2:9-10).
There is only one "Christian nation": the global people of God. The
very choice of terms such as *ecclesia* ("church"—but originally a Greek
term for the popular assembly) and *basilea* ("kingdom"—same Greek
word used for any political kingdom) ought to make this clear. This
"citizenship [that] is in heaven" (Phil 3:20) implies that we reside on
earth as "Christ's ambassadors" (2 Cor 5:20), "aliens and strangers"
(1 Pet 2:11). Cultivating a clear and precise awareness of this primary
political loyalty in the church is absolutely essential. (It is also why an
uncritical, worldly "patriotism" is so offensive in the church, and why
displays of flags and worldly political symbols in the church are such
a betrayal of the King we follow and of our fellow citizens residing
in other countries of the world.)

Denying worldly political powers any ultimate allegiance and re-
serving this only for God is the first positive step Christians may take

toward unmasking the demonic pretensions of the state and ordering their own political life in the world. The second step is a resolute refusal to conform to the sinful, oppressive ways and means of the worldly political arena. "Do not conform to the evil desires you had when you lived in ignorance" (1 Pet 1:14). "You were redeemed from the empty way of life handed down to you from your forefathers" (1 Pet 1:18). Not least, this means a renunciation of retaliation: "Do not repay evil with evil or insult with insult, but with blessing."

> Whoever would love life and see good days must keep his tongue from evil and his lips from deceitful speech. He must turn from evil and do good; he must seek peace and pursue it. For the eyes of the Lord are on the righteous and his ears are attentive to their prayer, but the face of the Lord is against those who do evil. (1 Pet 3:9-12)

There are *no* exception clauses for these instructions to Christians! They apply to politicians, voters and diplomats as much as business executives, students and homemakers. Any evil means in the political order must be fully rejected.

The third aspect of Peter's politics is to voluntarily, consistently, take the stance of a servant of others—even if this means being a suffering servant at times. "Submit [subordinate] yourselves for the Lord's sake to every authority instituted among men: whether to the king, as the supreme authority, or to governors, who are sent by him to punish those who do wrong and to commend those who do right. . . . Show proper respect to everyone: Love the brotherhood of believers, fear God, honor the king" (1 Pet 2:13-17). If we recall that Peter was probably writing this from Rome in the time of Nero, it is all the more significant that Peter calls for submission, honor and respect for the political rulers.

Fourth, however, is the call to "do the good and the right" as defined by God. Submission and servanthood never mean passivity or acquiescence in evil. Interwoven with the call to submission is the call to "live such good lives among the pagans that . . . they may see your good deeds and glorify God on the day he visits us" (1 Pet 2:12). "Live as free [people] . . . live as servants of God" (1 Pet 2:16). "It is God's will that by doing good you should silence the ignorant talk of [the] foolish" (1 Pet 2:15). Even if this results in unjust treatment, we are to commit ourselves to God and "continue to do good" (1 Pet 4:19).

In short, we must deny to the state any *absolute* allegiance, authority, obedience or worship, for this belongs only to God and his kingdom. We must rigorously eschew the evil tactics and means of the world (deceit, retaliation, insults), even if they are legal or customary in the political domain. As the free servants of God, we take the stance of servants in the world, subordinate rather than domineering. From that stance we seek to aggressively, lovingly, creatively carry out God's good in the world—even if we experience opposition and suffering. Christians who follow the politics of Peter will find in the long run that their faithfulness will prove more effective in arresting the growth of evil and in promoting good than any sort of compromise with the shortsighted politics of the world.[4]

The Fight against Disease and Death

Mammon and Babylon are ominous powers which must be combated by the faithful disciple. But their threat is often subtle and veiled. In contrast, the third front for "battling the powers" is always vivid and immediate: physical or psychological suffering and death. There can be no doubt that death is the great and final enemy. It was the terrible price of Adam and Eve's rebellion against God. It is the last enemy to be thrown in the "lake of fire." It was the great enemy which Jesus defeated in his death and resurrection. The disease, illness and disability from which we suffer is the intrusion of the hand of death in our life.

I will not repeat what has already been said about healing and exorcism in chapter three. Peter's activity as healer and exorcist in Acts flows directly out of the discipleship he learned at the side of Jesus of Nazareth. The problem of pain and suffering in the world is, of course, a great and complex mystery. There are at least three categories of suffering which we must note, though specific cases very often overlap these distinctions.[5]

In the first category is what I would call *pedagogical* suffering. This includes the ache of sore muscles after a good workout, the hunger pangs of a dieter, and the modest chastisements inflicted by parents on their children and by God on his people (see Heb 12:5-11). In every case this is intentional, limited and clearly connected with a beneficial result. Provided it does not spill over into the next two categories, this kind of suffering is not an enemy but a friend.

Second, there is *guilty* suffering. For example, the hangover after getting drunk, the heart trouble of the glutton, the cancer of the smoker, the poverty of the lazy, the marital wreckage of the adulterer, the auto accident of the reckless or drunk—these are species of suffering we bring on ourselves by our own folly.

Third, there is *innocent* suffering. This includes, for example, the victims of warfare and crime, and those suffering from blindness, disease, injury and hunger. Often this suffering results from other people's callousness or wickedness. It has nothing to do with any negligence on their part. The great problem of suffering is of this latter type. Nevertheless, even species of the second or first type can become demonic and oppressive.

None of this suffering was part of God's original creation; none of it will continue in God's new creation at the end of history (see Gen 1—2; Rev 21:1-4). It is not just a problem and a difficulty for human existence; it is an *enemy* against which we should fight. Death is *the* great enemy. Christians ought to declare war against suffering and death in the world.

There are two ways in which God's battle against demonic suffering and death takes place. First, many who are disabled, diseased or suffering are healed. The problem is frontally assaulted and defeated. The promise of the resurrection from the dead, guaranteed by the resurrection of Jesus himself, is the ultimate victory on this first front. Every sufferer can look forward to full healing for eternity.

Second, suffering can be stripped of its demonic power and inserted into a larger context in which it serves the good. Satan thought he defeated Jesus by killing him. It turned out, however, that this very death, by atoning for our sin, defeated Satan! Many Christians who have suffered have refused to be beaten by the "principalities and powers" and have created poetry, prose or other expressions of awesome depth and beauty in praise to God and assistance to other people. In these and other ways we can identify with Jesus Christ and share in his suffering in an important sense. Peter's first letter has a great deal to say about the joyful, glorious possibilities of turning innocent suffering into praise to God.

We have already observed how Peter battled against suffering and the threat of death in Acts. He was beaten, jailed, threatened, persecuted and locked up on death row. On two occasions he was victorious because an angel of the Lord delivered him out of prison. In other cases his tormenters left him with a bloodied body but also a joyful exultation that he had been able to be a faithful witness. Peter knew the subject of suffering from personal experience. He knew what it was to be chastised (type A suffering) by the Lord, he knew guilty suffering brought on by his own failures (type B), and in Acts, especially, he knew innocent suffering (type C). Sometimes he was miraculously delivered from his suffering; sometimes he deprived it of its demonic potential and turned it into praise to God.

Not long after his great Pentecost sermon, Peter and John were going up the steps of the temple for prayer, around 3 P.M. A beggar who had been crippled from birth and was now over forty years old called out for a donation as they passed. Peter stopped and said, "Silver and gold I do not have, but what I have I give you. In the name of Jesus Christ of Nazareth, walk" (Acts 3:6). Peter reached out a hand and pulled the man to his now-strengthened feet. The man walked, ran and leaped with glee! He praised God and clutched onto his new friend who had set him free. The people in the area quickly assembled together to observe this remarkable sight. They knew this man well, having seen him there whenever they went to the temple. Peter preached a sermon to the crowd, beginning with the disclaimer, "Men of Israel, why does this surprise you? Why do you stare at us as if by our own power or godliness we had made this man walk?" (Acts 3:12). Peter went on to explain that it was solely the power of the resurrected Christ that was responsible, in combination with the man's faith. You will recall from the previous chapter the story of Peter's arrest and imprisonment at the end of this sermon.

In Acts 5:14-16 many more healings and exorcisms are described:

More and more men and women believed in the Lord and were added to their number. As a result, people brought the sick into the streets and laid them on beds and mats so that at least Peter's shadow might fall on some of them as he passed by. Crowds gathered also from the towns around Jerusalem, bringing their sick and those tormented by evil spirits, and all of them were healed.

This precipitated another arrest by the Sanhedrin, another sermon by Peter, a flogging, and a grudging release on the advice of Gamaliel (Acts 5:17-42).

A few years later on a preaching tour through Lydda, thirty miles northwest of Jerusalem, Peter found among the Christians there a man named Aeneas who was paralyzed and bedridden for eight years. Peter said to him, "Aeneas, . . . Jesus Christ heals you. Get up and take care of your mat." Immediately he got up. Many of the residents of that area turned to the Lord as a result of this witness (Acts 9:34-35). When he arrived at Joppa, near the Mediterranean coast, Peter was ushered to the house of Dorcas ("Tabitha") a much-beloved woman of God who had just died of some illness. Her friends wept as they showed Peter some of the clothing she had made for the poor. Her body had been laid in an upper room of the house, and she would soon be buried. Peter asked everyone to leave the room and then knelt down and prayed. Turning to the body, Peter said, "Tabitha, get up." She opened her eyes, sat up, then took Peter's hand as he helped her stand up. Peter presented her alive to her overjoyed friends. Again, many people in the city were converted to Jesus Christ when they heard about the raising of Dorcas from the dead (Acts 9:36-42).

The four stories of Peter's healing activities in Acts culminate in the great miracle: raising someone who was dead. The correspondence between Peter's early experience, accompanying Jesus at the healing of Jairus's daughter, and this healing of Dorcas, is very close. On this occasion the Spirit of God was able to use Peter exactly as he had Jesus. From a low point of mouthing Satan's lie (at Caesarea Philippi), he had now reached a spectacular high point in his speaking and acting in the truth and power of God's Spirit.

These healings had value in their own right: just ask the person healed or the grieving friends! Compassion for the needy and afflicted is sufficient cause for the fight against disease and death. But for Peter these healings were also invariably centered on Jesus Christ. It was in his name and for his glory that the healing work was done. Peter never drew attention to himself as a "miracle worker" or "star." Just the opposite, he deflected all credit to Jesus Christ. In fact, it was his *teaching* about Jesus Christ that got him in trouble with the authorities. An independent miracle worker might be tolerable as an interesting diversion for the people. But when the miracles were linked with Jesus Christ, the people's fury was unleashed. Peter did not heal for his own glory or by his own strength. It was all in, through and for Jesus Christ. The result was that people were not only healed physically but spiritually: many people came to know Jesus through his work.

Once again, it bears repeating that we must neither dismiss this healing as an activity solely for the apostles and the primitive church, nor should we try to slavishly imitate and copy the exact forms we read about in Acts. Peter himself had no set "formula." One he helps with a hand, another he simply commands to rise, and beside another he kneels and prays. The consistent factors were the *effort* to heal and the intimate association with Jesus Christ. Thus we should worry less about the specific form our healing takes and rather use whatever means are available and appropriate to the service of Christ (prayer, medicine, surgery, nutrition, counseling and so on). The battle against the powers of death must continue in faithfulness to the call of Christ.[6]

Peter's first letter had a great deal to say about the subject of suffering. First, there was great stress on "doing good" in the world to the glory of God, and this certainly included the active effort to alleviate suffering. Second, Peter urged Christians to avoid bringing suffering on themselves by their own misdeeds and style of life (see 1 Pet 4:3, 15). Third, if we suffer innocently (especially for having taken a stand as a Christian), we should not only bear up under it and "cast all care upon the Lord," but even rejoice in what God is accomplishing through it—both for ourselves and for others.

It is terribly easy for Christians in an affluent society to settle into a comfortable existence in which Christian religion and piety are tame and reassuring. In an age of pluralism there is little cost attached to the profession of faith in Jesus Christ (or anyone else). There remain dark powers, however, which spread death in hospital beds, marriages, political structures and the economy. Their very subtlety is cause for increased vigilance. Death strikes quickly, but its hand may have been at work beneath the surface for a long time.

In particular, Peter (and Scripture as a whole) urges us to be aware of the "principalities and powers" which may exploit money, the state and ill health. Fight back! In the name of Jesus Christ, with whatever gifts and resources you have, struggle against the powers. Oppressed people can be set free. The proclamation of the Word of God accompanied by the performance of the acts of God is the one force capable of turning men and women from death to life.

For Reflection or Discussion

1. What has been your own philosophy of money and your economic goals? How are these related to biblical faith?

2. What is your political orientation, and how have you related this to your Christian commitment?

3. What kinds of suffering and pain do you encounter most frequently in your circle of work, neighborhood and church? What can be done to "heal" these sufferers?

11 A Faithful Shepherd: Ecumenicity and Church Discipline

"Be shepherds of God's flock that is under your care."

PETER'S EXPERIENCES IN ACTS CONCLUDE IN THREE EPISODES. FIRST IS THE story of Cornelius, the Roman centurion, converted during Peter's visit to his house. Luke gives a great deal of space to this affair (Acts 10:1—11:18) for it turned out to be decisively important in the history of Christianity. Second, Peter's imprisonment and subsequent escape from Herod Agrippa (discussed in the previous chapter) is detailed in Acts 12. Finally, in his last appearance in Acts, Peter plays a major role in the Council at Jerusalem (Acts 15)—a role based on his experience with Cornelius. These stories direct our attention to Peter's activity as a leader of the outward expansion of the church and its internal care. Peter's story in Acts comes to a brilliant conclusion as a model of church leadership.

Peter's experience with Cornelius and with church leadership calls attention to two of the besetting sins of the church over the centuries. These two problems are polar opposites of each other. On the one hand, some churches have been tempted to be undisciplined clubs of

"I'm okay, you're okay" ecumenists. Anybody and everybody is welcomed with no questions asked and little or no accountability. A
member might have been involved in a grotesque betrayal of the faith
just before arriving at the open arms of a church, or he or she might
commence such a betrayal while remaining in unquestioned good
standing—perhaps even an elder or deacon. While this policy at first
may seem like an admirable expression of love, it is precisely *unloving*.
It is *not* loving to endorse or acquiesce to a brother's or sister's self-
destructive (and community-destructive) behavior. Love means caring
enough to reach out and save this person from destroying their relationship with God and other people as well as their own self-respect.
Lack of discipline cannot be an expression of love for God. It is
nothing less than "cheap grace"—grace without repentance, grace
without discipleship—and a betrayal of the way of Jesus Christ.

On the other hand, many churches have fallen into the opposite
error of legalism and exclusivism. A good deal of the "looseness"
described in the previous paragraph has been inspired by the dread-
ful errors of would-be disciplinarians! A steady diet of withering criticism, cold rebukes, public humiliation, arrogance, pettiness and negativism is sufficient to explain why many Christians flee to looser
church environments or even totally abandon the church. It is little
short of astonishing how various little exclusive sects can boldly claim
to have preserved the pristine truth of the New Testament and then
pursue policies which make it almost impossible for anyone else to
share that "truth." There are few worse denials of the faith than for
a church to say to members of the body of Christ, for whom Jesus gave
his life, "we don't need you" (1 Cor 12:21-26) and cast them out of
the church or bar the doors to their entry. Those churches which
employ a rhetoric of ecumenicity but then practice legalistic, punitive
exclusivism add *hypocrisy* to the biblical indictment which they one day
will have to face.

But we are *all* guilty in one way or another. The churches of the
New Testament era itself had immediate problems with both "looseness" and "legalism," both ecumenicity and sectarianism. Nor is the
problem always one extreme or the other. More often than not, a
given church is unbiblically casual on some issues and unbiblically

repressive on others. In one church you may be silenced (or excommunicated) if you argue that the "rapture" will occur in the middle of the Great Tribulation instead of the beginning—but you can hold and teach any view of baptism you wish! In another church you may be disciplined if you dance to rock music—but you are free to lavish thousands of dollars on the latest Mercedes automobile and Paris fashions. Both of these examples are from churches I have attended. But I have also attended churches where the exact opposite was the case; for example, baptism was well-defined, eschatological details were left open, simple lifestyles were encouraged and dancing was optional![1]

Are these absurd situations really the "church built on the rock"? Well, yes and no. Yes, the church remains the church of Jesus Christ despite its absurdities and abysmal failures. Like Peter, like the church at Corinth, both individual disciples and churches are made out of ordinary people who are spectacular in defeat and buffoonery as well as when they display the presence of God's amazing grace. God accepts people (and churches) like Jacob, like Peter. But no, it is not good enough to be satisfied with any combination of looseness or exclusivism. No matter how emphatically our tradition says to keep doing what has been done before in our churches, we *must* seek to grow in faithfulness to the call of Christ. It is only when we refuse to grow that we will die. As long as there is life and intent to improve, Christ will be among us.

Cornelius: The Outsider (Acts 10)
Cornelius was the outsider whose entry into the early Christian church epitomized both the promise and the challenge of "ecumenicity" (by which I mean biblically faithful "inclusiveness" on a broad scale). Cornelius was a Gentile, not a Jew. He was, moreover, an employee and representative of Rome, the despised, imperialist colonial power holding Palestine under its thumb. Still worse, he was a military leader, stationed in the invader's main camp, Caesarea, the Roman capital of Judea. In contrast to all of this, the earliest church was predominantly Jewish, pacifist and centered in Jerusalem.

There were, of course, certain movements toward crossing these barriers during Jesus' own ministry. He was worshiped at his birth by "wise men" from the East (Mt 2). Jesus healed another Roman centurion's servant at Capernaum (Lk 7:4-5). He reached out to the mixed-race Samaritans (see Jn 4). The appointment of a group of seventy representatives was a signal to his followers that his good news was for all seventy nations of the world (as Jewish tradition counted them—Lk 10:1-24). His great commission clearly called for extension beyond Judea and Samaria to "all nations" (Lk 24:47).

Two of the most intransigent barriers dividing people of that era were effectively being broken down: the class divisions between rich and poor, free and slave, and the gender division between male and female. Women were the recipients of the Holy Spirit prophesied by Joel, just as men. Although subsequent generations were to repress women once again in the church, a sweeping revolution of freedom and sexual equality took place in the first-century church. So, too, a propertied man like Barnabas labored side by side in equality with ordinary fishermen like Peter. Other divisions of age and education were also being overcome.

One major barrier remained solid: the racial, cultural, political and religious wall of separation between Jews and Gentiles. In our own era anti-Semitism and pro-Semitism continue to be a cancer in the human race, as tensions in the Middle East, the Soviet Union and the abominable Holocaust in Nazi Germany bear ample witness. Other species of the same basic phenomenon deeply divide Blacks, Caucasians, Hispanics, Asians, American Indians and others. Racial and cultural divisions constitute one of the supreme tests of the power of the Christian message. These alienations are as difficult to heal as the worst disease or disability. Racism and cultural prejudice are as demonic as Mammon or Babylon. Satan is the divider.

No matter what Jewish Christians might have thought at the time, the story of Cornelius proved that God was at work in the life of an "outsider." Cornelius was "devout and God-fearing; he gave generously to those in need and prayed to God regularly" (Acts 10:2). He was a genuine seeker for the truth about God and for the presence of God. It is possible that his interest in Christianity had been fanned indirectly by the work of Philip the evangelist. Philip had visited Caesarea on his preaching tour after his remarkable encounter near Gaza with an Ethiopian court official who turned to Jesus Christ (Acts 8:26-40).

In a vision God urged Cornelius to send messengers to nearby Joppa to invite Peter for a visit. Cornelius immediately sent two servants and one of his soldiers who was also a devout seeker. Twenty-four hours later, the messengers delivered their invitation to Peter. After spending the night at Simon the Tanner's place in Joppa, Peter and the three friends of Cornelius headed for Caesarea, accompanied by six other Christians. By the time he arrived, Cornelius had assembled a group of relatives and close friends to hear him. When Peter entered the house, Cornelius fell down "in reverence," but Peter quickly made him get up and said, "Stand up, . . . I am only a man myself" (Acts 10:26). After exchanging their stories of how God had guided each of them to this meeting, Cornelius introduced Peter's talk by saying, "Now we are all here in the presence of God to listen to everything the Lord has commanded you to tell us" (10:33).

As Peter was concluding his talk, "the Holy Spirit came on all who heard the message," and they began "speaking in tongues and praising God," in a kind of gentile day of Pentecost (10:44-46). The same kind of miracle of communication that had taken place in Jerusalem earlier occurred among this Roman group of gentile believers. Peter then baptized the believers in water to symbolize their identification with Jesus Christ in repentance and faith. Cornelius and friends "asked Peter to stay with them for a few days," during which Peter undoubtedly filled them in on many more details of the Christian way of discipleship, individually as well as in the church.

The point of the story of Cornelius is clear. First, God *does* work among outsiders, even the farthest removed from our own subculture and church. It is a terrible mistake to assume that God only speaks to "me," to "my kind of people" or in "my kind of church." Second, what God accepts and rewards is the search for his truth and presence. The letter to the Hebrews puts it this way: "Anyone who comes to [God] must believe that he exists and that he rewards those who earnestly seek him" (Heb 11:6). Third, it is God's intention to give the full gift of his Spirit to everyone who comes to him with simple faith in Jesus Christ.

All of this implies an aggressive, ecumenical outreach and spirit in our churches. If God accepts and speaks to anyone who seeks him, what gives his followers the right to discourage, ignore or (worst of all) reject such seekers? If God rewards simple repentance and faith in Jesus Christ with the full and spectacular gifts of his Spirit, what gives his followers the right to hold back in any way or place additional conditions on their acceptance into full fellowship among us? Our churches ought to be places where all outsiders, cultural deviants and social misfits are warmly welcomed, provided only that they are true seekers after Jesus Christ.

The Old Guard (Acts 11, 15)

Unfortunately, such an ecumenical policy did not (and still does not) sit well with some members of the church and its leadership. A well-meaning but grumpy "old guard" reacted against "undesirable elements" coming into their "homogenous church-growth unit." "The apostles and the brothers throughout Judea heard that the Gentiles also had received the word of God. So when Peter went up to Jerusalem, the circumcised believers criticized him and said, 'You went into the house of uncircumcised men and ate with them' " (Acts 11:1-3). Even though Peter succeeded in communicating the joy of this series of events, it proved to be only a matter of time before the old guard again began leaning on Peter and others to resume the old traditions and not eat with Gentiles, even those in the church (Gal 2). Apparently even James, the Lord's brother and a pillar in the Jerusalem church leadership, was guilty of this repressive, exclusivist reaction. Still later, the council of Jerusalem was provoked by members of the old guard who insisted that Gentiles coming into the church should have to be circumcised in accordance with Jewish tradition (Acts 15:1-5).[2]

In a brilliant phrase, a recent author has said that the "seven last words of the church" are: "We never did it that way before!"[3] The rules governing circumcision and diet had been important and meaningful in the past. The problem was clinging to them when they were no longer helpful or applicable. The power of legalism and traditionalism was such that sincere leaders could conveniently forget (or perhaps rationalize away) their Lord's own setting aside of traditional food laws (Mk 7:18-19) and the memory of the charge that "this man welcomes sinners and eats with them" (Lk 15:2). Instead of rejoicing in the expansion of the gospel and in the breaking of barriers dividing people, the old-guard leadership grumbled in criticism and a misguided attempt to clamp down on the work of God.

A Faithful Shepherd (Acts 10, 11, 15)

A third factor, beside *the outsider* and *the old guard,* was Peter himself, who became a model of *the faithful shepherd* and leader. Peter's role as a leader can be examined in terms of three relationships: to God, to the outsider and to the old guard. Peter himself needed to be prepared for faithful presence in this situation by a relationship to God. Good and faithful church leadership was not,· for Peter, the result of completing a course in management training in Athens. God may very well use gifts and experiences gained outside of the church, but the stress in New Testament teaching about church leadership is on spirituality and a wisdom that comes from walking with God (1 Tim 3; Tit 1).

It was when he was praying that God prepared Peter for his encounter with Cornelius, an outsider whom he (just as much as the old guard) was disinclined to seek or accept. Peter had a vision while on the housetop of Simon the tanner, where he had gone for his afternoon prayer time. In his vision, he saw heaven open up and something like a great sheet descending toward earth with all kinds of animals in it—both kosher and otherwise. A voice ordered him, "Get up, Peter. Kill and eat." (Peter, by the way, was hungry and about to go downstairs to eat when this happened!) Peter objected, "Surely not, Lord! I have never eaten anything impure or unclean." The voice responded, "Do not call anything impure that God has made clean." This happened three times before the sheet full of animals disappeared and the vision was over (Acts 10:9-16).

Peter's initial perplexity about the meaning of this vision was clarified when the messengers of Cornelius arrived and explained the invitation to come to Caesarea. By the time he arrived at Cornelius's house, Peter could say, "You are well aware that it is against our law for a Jew to associate with a Gentile or visit him. But God has shown me that I should not call any man impure or unclean. So when I was sent for, I came without raising any objection" (Acts 10:28-29). After Cornelius shared his own vision with Peter, Peter replied, "I now realize how true it is that God does not show favoritism but accepts [people] from every nation who fear him and do what is right" (10:34-35). Peter then gave a clear summary of the gospel of Jesus Christ. When the Holy Spirit fell on the new believers, he warmly welcomed them into the fellowship and baptized them.

What does it take to make a good leader? Peter was first of all a man of prayer who had a close walk with God. He was a man open to hearing the voice of God. The fact that his vision was repeated three times in a row must have made him realize that it was a decisively important point in his development. At his worst moment he had denied Christ three times. In the critical moment of his comeback to Christ, he had been challenged three times about his love for Christ and commissioned three times to feed and care for God's flock. Peter was not just open to hearing God repeat lessons he had heard before. He was a leader ready to grow and change as God might want him to. He was not only willing to accept a new idea, he was willing to act on it. He was humble, willing to share—even with the outsiders whom his tradition had led him to avoid. He directed all attention to Jesus Christ. He rejoiced in the great new thing God was doing. He confirmed his acceptance of the outsiders by staying with them a few days. It is this kind of leadership that the church so sorely needs today: spirituality, growth, learning and obedience to God; humility and Jesus-centered servanthood toward outsiders.

But Peter is also a model in his relations to the old guard. Confronted by criticism he did not respond with denunciations such as, "Though all of you are racist exclusivists, I will never be!" Rather, Peter gave them a calm retelling of the whole story of his lesson from God and the subsequent marvel of the Spirit's work at Cornelius's house. He concluded, "If God gave them the same gift as he gave us, who believed in the Lord Jesus Christ, who was I to think that I could oppose God?" When they heard this, they were silenced. And they "praised God, saying, 'So then, God has granted even the Gentiles repentance unto life' " (Acts 11:1-18).

Peter responded to criticism not by ignoring it and avoiding trouble—the issue was too important. Nor did he take a position in any way superior to his critics. He heard their complaints, went to them and gave calm persuasive testimony to what God had done. "If you are offering your gift at the altar and there remember that your brother has something against you, leave your gift there in front of the altar. First go and be reconciled to your brother; then come and offer your gift" (Mt 5:23-24). Jesus' teaching and Peter's example remain valid today. Many acrimonious disputes would be avoided if leaders (and other disciples) would make quick, humble attempts at achieving reconciliation.

Peter's reconciliation (his vindication, in fact) came about by a report of a work of Jesus Christ. It is always easier to argue against theories than brute reality, especially the reality of Christ. The critics were silenced by the *fact* that God had accepted Cornelius, not by a novel theory that the church ought to start a new program of outreach to Roman military commanders who liked eating pork! Likewise, today it is much easier for a church (old guard and all) to commit itself to a ministry if there is clear evidence that God is already at work in the seeds of such a ministry. It is stronger, for example, to have a born-again drug addict praising God in your midst than to argue in committee meetings that the church should reach out to drug addicts!

Round one went to Peter, Cornelius and the Lord, who reaches out to outsiders! Round two was much rougher. The old guard in Jerusalem lost its enthusiasm for the full acceptance of Gentiles. They began pressuring Peter, Barnabas and others to reinstate the divisive old food laws and stop eating with Gentiles. Peter "began to draw back and separate himself from the Gentiles because he was afraid of those who belonged to the circumcision group." Paul, who reported this in his letter to the Galatians, stepped in at Antioch and opposed Peter "to his face, because he was clearly in the wrong" (Gal 2:11-12). Peter had been intimidated, after all, by the old guard. Paul was right, and he confronted Peter face to face. The two brothers in Christ were reconciled, and Peter turned around again. Even the greatest leaders make mistakes!

The Council at Jerusalem (Acts 15)

Barnabas and Peter came back in line with Paul and with God's ecumenical plan. In coming months and years, however, the narrow
exclusivist position continued to be argued. Some teachers from Judea
pressed the case that no one could be saved who refused to be circumcised in accordance with ancient Jewish law (Acts 15:1). This time
Paul and Barnabas were unable to convince the old-guard tradition-
alists and a council of "apostles and elders met to consider this question" in Jerusalem (15:6).

"After much debate," Peter stood up and, in his final appearance
in the pages of Acts, made a powerful presentation:

"Brothers, you know that some time ago God made a choice among
you that the Gentiles might hear from my lips the message of the
gospel and believe. God, who knows the heart, showed that he
accepted them by giving the Holy Spirit to them, just as he did to
us. He made no distinction between us and them, for he purified
their hearts by faith. Now then, why do you try to test God by
putting on the necks of the disciples a yoke that neither we nor our
fathers have been able to bear? No! We believe it is through the
grace of the Lord Jesus that we are saved, just as they are." (Acts
15:7-11)

All debate was silenced by this great witness of the veteran leader.
After Paul and Barnabas related their stories of what God had done
among the Gentiles, James, who had previously been active in the old
guard, drew together a pastorally sensitive conclusion: no burden
should be placed on the Gentiles except to "abstain from food pol-
luted by idols, from sexual immorality, from the meat of strangled
animals and from blood." Nothing more was to be said about "not
eating with Gentiles," "circumcision is required for salvation," and so
on. The decision was communicated by letter and by personal messengers. The Christian "flock" rejoiced at this decision!

Peter's role was to provoke an agreement, a reconciliation. He had
been one of the first great agents of outreach to the Gentiles. Now
he was the one who closed a bitter debate with words that led to an
overcoming of alienation. The result was a church that was ecumenical and open—yet disciplined. The "keys to the kingdom" were used

to open the door wide to entry by non-Jews. The responsibility to "bind and loose" was exercised by coming to consensus in a practical judgment. As Paul was to put it later in his letter to Rome, food means nothing in itself. But care must be taken not to let one person's freedom become a stumbling block to the consciences of brothers and sisters (Rom 14). In this case, the food laws had become part of a very threatening, divisive situation. Rather than permitting a "to each his own" individualism, the leadership promulgated a wise rule for community peace.

The issues that divide vary over the centuries and from place to place. Certain matters are negotiable. Others require a firm stand. In this case, sexual purity and the full acceptance of other races into fellowship were the permanent factors to which attention was drawn. But to preserve the peace and unity of the body of Christ, certain secondary issues of an extremely divisive nature had to be "bound" by community decision as well. A wise accommodation was made, and then enforced, to the joyful gratitude of the people of God.

For our own era, a twofold agenda is implied. First, our churches must reach out aggressively across the lines which divide "insiders" from "outsiders." It is the loving unity of brothers and sisters from many and diverse backgrounds which is the most powerful apologetic for the truth of the gospel. A narrow, exclusive, homogeneous church lacks not only a great opportunity to bear witness to the work of Christ, but is itself internally impoverished for lack of the diverse gifts of the body of Christ. We must ask what are the divisions which ravage our neighborhoods, cities, regions and even our churches. We need leaders who will catch the vision of reaching across those barriers. We need to use those "keys of the kingdom" to fling open the gates to the kingdom of heaven for all to come in repentance and faith to Jesus Christ.

Second, we need churches with the courage and wisdom to take on the task of "binding and loosing." When it comes to matters such as racism, violence, adultery, lying and other nonnegotiables, we need leaders who will lovingly, faithfully insist on maintaining justice and love in the high ethical standards we know in Jesus Christ. Anything less is not only a betrayal of Christ and a quenching of the Spirit, it is an acquiescence in the slavery and self-destruction of wayward disciples. The church is a place to set people free from their slaveries, not to leave them in bondage.

The church must also seek with courage and wisdom to "bind and loose" various secondary issues, insofar as these threaten the unity of the body of Christ. This means that various "old guards" sometimes need to loosen up rather than forcing an outworn traditionalism and legalism on the flock. But it also means that others of a "looser" bent will need to move toward greater care and sensitivity on issues which are serious stumbling blocks to others. I am by no means suggesting that every issue needs the attention and verdict of church leadership! But when an issue is deeply divisive and threatening, the responsibility to "bind and loose" ought faithfully to be carried out.

While this discussion of leadership has particular relevance for "official" church leadership, it is also important for all disciples. This is so, first of all, because it is important to understand, appreciate and encourage those who serve us to faithfully carry out their tasks of leadership. If we are called on to "recognize" or even elect such leaders, we should keep the biblical qualifications and expectations firmly in mind and not be swayed by the worldly status or professional role played by a given individual. An undistinguished fisherman may be a better elder than a banking executive in some cases!

But it is also the case that every disciple is called to exercise servant-leadership in one way or another. All disciples, young and old, should find others to care for and shepherd, even in a very unofficial capacity. Obviously parents relate as leaders to their children. Teachers relate as leaders to their students. Teen-agers ought to reach out to their peers and to younger members of the congregation with positive, caring, humble leadership.

Thus, Peter's advice to "shepherds" ought to be taken seriously not just by official "elders" but by everyone. "Be shepherds of God's flock that is under your care, serving as overseers—not because you must, but because you are willing, as God wants you to be; not greedy for money, but eager to serve; not lording it over those entrusted to you, but being examples to the flock. And when the Chief Shepherd appears, you will receive the crown of glory that will never fade away"

(1 Pet 5:2-4). The task of leadership is to care for *God's* flock, not to possess it as our own. Willingness and eagerness to take on this task is what God asks for, not a grudging spirit. A strategy of servanthood and leadership by example is called for, not a domineering "lording it over" those in our care. This is how, many years later, Peter interpreted the call of Jesus to "feed my lambs" and "tend my flock."

Unquestionably, we also need John's great passages describing the work of Jesus as the "good shepherd" (Jn 10). We need Paul's rich teaching on the church and its leadership (especially in Ephesians and in the letters to Timothy and Titus). We are helped a great deal by studying Paul's approach to the terrible problems wracking the Corinthian church. But in an era ravaged by strife among those of different race, class, gender, education and age, in an era where churches continue to be plagued both by casual, loose ecumenicity and tight, hard-nosed exclusivism, we do well to take another close look at the leadership of Peter. His weakness (as well as his strength) gives us hope that God might use even imperfect disciples like ourselves to assist in leading the church toward greater faithfulness, to the glory of our Lord Jesus Christ.

For Reflection or Discussion

1. What are the divisions among Christians—and among people in general—that most deeply trouble you today? What might be done to heal them?

2. What have been your experiences with "loose ecumenism" or "narrow exclusivism"? What caused these situations to develop? Could anything be done to correct the situation to a more biblical balance?

3. What have been your experiences in Christian leadership—either official or unofficial? Where are your opportunities for servant leadership now?

12 Hope & Truth: The Message of the Letters

"Be on your guard so that you may not be carried away by . . . error. . . .
But grow in the grace and knowledge of our Lord and Savior Jesus Christ."

IF WE HAD ONLY THE MATERIAL ON PETER FROM THE GOSPELS, ACTS AND Paul's letters, we would already have good reason for paying attention to his teaching and example. However, we also have two letters in the New Testament bearing his name. In these letters we are given Peter's mature reflection on the Christian way—at least thirty years after he began following Jesus and at least fifteen years after the Council at Jerusalem (the last story about him in Acts). Throughout the preceding studies, we have drawn on relevant sections of these later letters to try to incorporate Peter's mature thought on each topic considered. The letters are not, however, just "catalogs" of mature Petrine perspectives; they are each literary wholes, and deserve to be studied as such. They provide not just the most mature Peter but the most "synoptic" and orderly presentation of his thought. Finally, both letters address particular problems and, thus, illuminate yet two other aspects of Christian existence.

From what perspectives may we best understand these letters? For

Christians, of course, these letters have been recognized as part of the canon, the Word of God. Looming also in the background are Peter's own personal experiences, the rich and multifaceted life we have examined in previous chapters. Thus two questions that can always be raised in reading these letters are: (1) What might God be trying to say to us in this letter? and (2) How does this letter illuminate and complete Peter's story of Christian discipleship?

The rest of the background is more difficult to know or describe with great precision. The evidence both inside and outside the New Testament is not very complete. However, a probable (or at least possible) scenario runs as follows: Though he played a key role in the early leadership of the church in Jerusalem, Peter was, by temperament and calling, a better roving missionary and ambassador for Jesus Christ than a leader of a fixed congregation. He soon began traveling to Lydda, Joppa, Caesarea, Antioch and elsewhere. Especially after his miraculous escape from Herod Agrippa's prison in the early forties (Acts 12), Peter seems to have moved around outside of Jerusalem, mostly concentrating on a mission to the Jews (Gal 2). After Peter, James, the Lord's brother, became the most prominent resident leader in Jerusalem until he was executed in A.D. 62.

Because of the explicit address of the first letter and the statement in 2 Peter that this was the "second letter" written to the audience, it seems that in his travels Peter developed a particularly important relationship with the churches in northern Asia Minor. His travels probably also took him to Corinth and perhaps elsewhere in Greece. It appears that Peter ended his career in Rome (the "Babylon" of 1 Pet 5:13) with Paul, Mark, Silvanus (Silas) and others. Strong tradition has it that Peter died as a martyr in Rome in the persecution Nero launched in the summer of A.D. 64.

Early historical voices (and perhaps some internal stylistic considerations) argue that Peter, while in Rome in the early sixties, gave Mark the bulk of the material for Mark's Gospel. At the same time, I believe, Peter received word that his long-time friends in the churches of northern Asia Minor were threatened by growing persecution for their faith. Assisted by Silvanus (his amanuensis, or editorial/secretarial assistant) Peter carefully prepared his first letter. Not long after finishing and sending this letter, Peter may have heard a new, more discouraging report that the same churches were falling prey to certain false teachers—maybe because their "revised version" of discipleship escaped persecution. In light of this, Peter prepared the material for a second letter, drawing partly on Jude's letter about false teaching (or a third tract on which both Peter and Jude depended). He was assisted by a new amanuensis with a literary style radically different from that of Silvanus. Whether this second letter was finished and sent immediately, or edited and sent after Peter's martyrdom, we do not know for sure. In the judgment of the church, however, this second letter was also inspired, authoritative teaching on the Christian way and was included in our New Testament.

Hope in Difficult Times (1 Peter)

The most striking feature of 1 Peter is the amount of attention Peter gives to the threat and fact of suffering—especially suffering as a result of faithfulness to Jesus Christ. The audience to which he wrote was facing this challenge in a very pronounced fashion. In many parts of the world today (and in the past), faithful Christians face overt and sustained persecution. For them, the message of 1 Peter has direct and immediate application. But 1 Peter is also important for Christians in the more tolerant, liberal democratic West, because (1) things might someday change for the worse, and we need to be prepared, and (2) in our global era not a few Western Christians may find themselves, by choice or assignment, living and working in a less hospitable part of the world.

Suffering, however, is not just a function of external oppressors. It is also a function of Christian faithfulness in a world separated and alienated from Jesus Christ. Even if we in the West *never* face opposition or hardship, the reason may just have as much to do with our understanding and practice of discipleship as with the external political climate. First Peter implicitly puts in question such discipleship. Have we softened or removed the cross and sacrificial servanthood from our discipleship? Have we become expert as "finessing" the potential conflicts and avoiding the reproach of Christ? Suffering is never to be sought; it has no intrinsic value. But some self-critical inquiry is called for by 1 Peter. Maybe our comfortable existence owes itself to an inadvertent neglect of biblical faithfulness.

But suppose we *are* experiencing some kind of persecution or suffering for our discipleship: for example, sarcasm, verbal attacks and rejection by roommates, relatives, colleagues or schoolmates who discover we are Christians; ostracism, injustice in grading or job promotions when we insist on living by Christian standards of truthfulness, justice and righteousness; abuse from cowards who take advantage of our voluntary servanthood, peacemaking and nonretaliation; personal anguish at losing someone or foregoing something we badly want but cannot take without compromising our commitment to Christ. In these and other cases of suffering for Christ, how do we respond? What do we say to ourselves or to others who are faced with such tests and trials?

For Peter, the response had five parts. Whether we are personally faced with some kind of suffering, trying to assist a brother or sister so tested or, more generally, preparing Christians for discipleship in a difficult world, these five points are important food for Christian growth and strength.

E. G. Selwyn, *the* modern expert on 1 Peter, describes 1 Peter as "a microcosm of Christian faith and duty, the model of a pastoral charge," addressed to Christians in a difficult time.

> The purpose of the letter is to exhort and encourage them in a time of trial; and this he does by unfolding to them the ways of God as revealed in the Gospel, by recalling them to the example of Christ, and by expounding the principles of conduct . . . which were inherent in their calling and their baptism.[1]

The first point is to clarify the meaning of our conversion and our personal relationship with Jesus Christ (1 Pet 1:1—2:3). Especially when facing difficult circumstances, we may wonder about the meaning and value of our Christian life. At that point it is important to go back to certain basics. Becoming a disciple of Jesus is the start of a totally new kind of life characterized by faith, hope and love. A disciple becomes, in a profound sense, a "stranger" in the world—an adventure which is both joyful and (sometimes) painful. In the quest to "be holy as God is holy" (that is, different like God), Peter stresses the importance of two aspects of basic Christian living. Especially in difficult times, the Christian must make every effort to be closely, vitally attached to Jesus Christ, the Word of God. Equally important is to realize the extent to which God has attached himself to us! Surviving joyfully in time of trial means seizing on to our Lord, and it means resting in the confidence that God the Father, Son and Holy Spirit has chosen us, blessed us and adopted us into his family. These two angles on the meaning of our conversion to Christ are essential to preparing disciples for tough circumstances.

Second, not only are disciples to tenaciously follow their Lord (and live in the freedom and confidence of God's choice of them), they must also tenaciously live, worship and witness within the people of God—the new "temple," the new "priesthood," the new "nation" (1 Pet 2:4-12). Christ makes his presence felt as the cornerstone of the corporate "building"—not just as the Lord of the individual. The Holy Spirit dwells in the corporate "temple"—not just in the heart of the individual. More than ever, tough, threatening times require a group effort. An isolated, individual disciple is extremely vulnerable.

The third stage of Peter's preparation of disciples for difficult times is his review of the meaning of servanthood in relationships—to the political powers, to masters or bosses, to one's spouse and to others in the community of faith (1 Pet 2:11—3:12). In every case (as we have seen earlier), the strategy includes (a) nonconformity to the evil in the world around us, (b) a voluntary assumption of the stance of a subordinate servant rather than trying to dominate and coerce others, and (c) a continual pattern of "doing the right and the good," as defined by God. It is by means of this strategy, closely modeled on Jesus, especially his death and resurrection, that disciples overcome the world, often winning over those who initially opposed them.

Fourth, Peter addresses head-on the issue of suffering and opposition (1 Pet 3:13—4:19). If there is opposition, he argues, we must be sure it is not due to our own stupidity or unfaithfulness, but truly because we are doing what is good and right. The servanthood strategy may win over our persecutors; giving a good account verbally of our hope may also help. Still, even after our best efforts, unjust suffering may be our lot. Cultivating a deeper love for our brothers and sisters, practicing servanthood, cultivating hope in God's coming kingdom, developing endurance, patience and prayer, identifying with the crucified Lord and maintaining a firm commitment of our lives and circumstances to God—these are the appropriate responses to unavoidable suffering for being faithful and doing right.

Finally, Peter concludes with a call for servant leaders like Jesus (the "Chief Shepherd"), genuine humility in interpersonal relations, and daily trust and confidence in God's care (1 Pet 5:1-14). Behind all opposition and persecution of our faith, it is our "enemy, the devil," who is prowling "around like a roaring lion, looking for someone to devour" (1 Pet 5:8). Peter's letter closes with a call to be alert, self-controlled and ready to actively "resist him . . . firm in [our] faith." We are involved in a spiritual combat. We may be bloodied in this struggle, but God will never let go of his chosen people. Faced with the worst sort of persecution, a Christian can know that God will win out in the end, and that we will share in that final victory. And for the day-to-day struggle there is a strategy for a faithful, hopeful, joyful, peaceful life in the presence of both God and our brothers and sisters.

Fighting for the Truth (2 Peter)

The purpose of 2 Peter is clearly to rally Christians threatened by false teaching.[2] In 1 Peter the challenge of persecution arose from those outside the community of faith. In 2 Peter another challenge arises within the community. These two situations appear to be inversely related throughout much of our history. That is, persecution (while regrettable) often purifies the faith and teaching of the church; toleration (while desirable) often leads to a flowering of false teaching of various kinds.[3] In our own era in the West, religious freedom has been accompanied by a proliferation of heresies and deformations of the Christian faith. Almost any opinion or practice can be (and has been!) promoted somewhere, sometime, in the name of Christ.

Second Peter alerts us to the problem: "There were also false prophets among the people [of Israel], just as there will be false teachers among you" (2 Pet 2:1). "Be on your guard so that you may not be carried away by their error" (2 Pet 3:17). A reading of 2 Peter does not suggest a "live and let live" position in the face of false teaching! And this is not just a problem of ignorant, uneducated heretics—it is a question also of those who are recognized teachers and leaders. Peter certainly pulls no punches in identifying and publicly denouncing the heresies and falsehoods, and in strong language. This sort of response may be called for at times. However, Peter does not counsel his audience to throw its energy into fiery rhetoric or even theological trials of leaders. He proposes a counterattack, but of a different nature.[4]

False teaching comes in a thousand varieties, and it is often difficult to determine whether a somewhat unusual opinion is a threat to the apostolic faith or a legitimate exercise of freedom of thought and conviction. Not infrequently, "heresy hunters" have made mistakes and gone too far. Thus, it is helpful to identify the problems that 2 Peter regards as important enough to be resisted.

First, the core and basis of the false teaching is that they deny "the Sovereign Lord who bought them"—in fact, they "despise authority" (2 Pet 2:1, 10).[5] There was a great claim to knowledge, but the ideas and proposals of the false teachers did not square with the rule of Jesus Christ. Jesus Christ the Lord is the standard of all truth. This is the issue that most deserves our attention and is most worth fighting for.

Second, a great deal of Peter's denunciation of the false teachers in 2 Peter has to do with their ethics, the way they live, the relation of their teaching to daily life. Despite their claims to special knowledge of God, they are dividing and destroying the community (the original meaning of *heresy* has to do with "splitting" and "dividing") and practicing and promoting renewed slavery to greed, dishonesty, adultery and various other forms of depravity. Heresy and false teaching, then, concern not just ideas and doctrines but the way we live. We must make decisions about various "trees" by the kind of "fruit" they bear in life.

Third, a particular emphasis is placed on their denial of Christ's return. Among the false teachers are scoffers who undermine confidence in the promise that Jesus will come again in grace and judgment. Peter's Christianity was an eschatological faith and life. It takes place in a history that is moving to a great culmination and consummation: God's new creation. It is a life permeated and guided by hope, by an orientation to God's future. An attack on this hope is not to be taken lightly.

This is only the barest outline of Peter's identification of "false teaching worth resisting," but it can help orient us in the conflicts of our own epoch. Equally important is the strategy of resistance counseled by 2 Peter. Chief in importance is the call to "grow in the grace and knowledge of our Lord and Savior Jesus Christ" (2 Pet 3:18). We will best be able to recognize error when we know the truth well. We will be able to resist false teaching that denies the Lord when we know that Lord well. Thus, it is more important to become experts in the way and teaching of our Lord than to become experts in the multi-faceted catalog of errors, counterfeits and heresies. Implicit in this task is careful attention to the witness of the true prophets and apostles in Scripture.

Christians must also "make every effort" to grow ethically—that is, to grow from faith to love in a life that manifests God's truth. In a brilliant passage, Peter says: "Add to your faith goodness [moral virtue or excellence]; and to goodness, knowledge [prudence, moral discernment]; and to knowledge, self-control [temperance]; and to self-control, perseverance [courage]; and to perseverance, godliness; and to godliness, brotherly kindness; and to brotherly kindness, love" (2 Pet 1:5-7). "If you do these things," Peter says, "you will never fall" (2 Pet 1:10). The starting point of this series is faith, received "through the righteousness [justice] of our God and Savior Jesus Christ" (2 Pet 1:1). All too often, Christians have either ignored the problem of a Christian ethic guiding daily life or they have simply adopted an ethical system from the world. For 2 Peter neither approach will do. Peter stresses the critical importance of ethical guidance and formation in an environment of false teaching. But what is also fascinating is the way Peter seizes, modifies and subordinates to the gospel the four classical ethical virtues of justice, prudence, temperance and courage. Space prohibits further exploration of this text here, but we must note the richness and promise of Peter's call to an evangelical ethic.[6]

Finally, 2 Peter calls Christians to a robust, life-changing hope in the return of Jesus Christ and the coming of the kingdom of God. It is the Lord's patience which explains the delay of his return, but he will keep his promise. For Peter this is not an escapist or otherworldly dogma. It draws together the preceding two points: the knowledge of Jesus Christ and the effort to live an evangelically ethical life. The anticipation of Jesus' return inspires and shapes our present existence.

> You ought to live holy and godly lives as you look forward to the day of God and speed its coming. . . . In keeping with his promise we are looking forward to a new heaven and a new earth, the home of righteousness.
>
> So then, dear friends, since you are looking forward to this, make every effort to be found spotless, blameless and at peace with him. (2 Pet 3:11-14)

To respond to false teaching simply in intellectual terms is not enough. It is not enough to "add to your faith the theological analysis of heresy"! We must add to our faith virtue, culminating in a life of sacrificial love. The power of a transformed life exceeds that of a sharpened tongue in the combat against error and falsehood. False teaching is a continuing problem in our era. A major component in our fight for the truth is the discovery of an eschatological ethic to help us live and think in daily life, always guided by the knowledge of our Lord Jesus Christ and fired by a deep hope in the coming kingdom of God.

Peter's Message for the Twentieth Century

Peter looms across the New Testament as no other figure—except Jesus Christ. Peter may be the best key to our understanding of the diversity, unity and development of apostolic Christianity. His experience ranges across the spectrum of theological and ethical issues from conversion to apologetics, from ecclesiology to eschatology. His experiences range from great victories to terrible defeats, from the reckless risk of faith to a cowardly denial of the faith. His letters provide a carefully constructed, pastoral encouragement to persevere in spite of opposition and suffering, and a flaming denunciation of false teaching within the church.

Peter is not the whole story, of course. We need Paul, Moses, John and all the rest of the prophets and apostles. So, too, my own study with its conclusions is not enough: each reader must evaluate what I have said in light of Scripture and with the assistance of other voices in the body of Christ. This is one more word on New Testament Christianity. It certainly is not the last word.

By way of conclusion, though, let me briefly review what I believe Simon Peter can teach us:

1. Christian *conversion* is the entering into a personal, living relationship with Jesus Christ. However simply one understands Jesus, the new disciple repudiates his or her old sinful orientation (repentance) and takes the first step of a life committed to following Jesus, believing that he is Savior, Lord and God. It is an event which may culminate a long, patient process of seeking to know this Jesus. It is an event that claims the whole of our daily life and work, not just our "religious activities." It is filled with hope and promise—a veritable "new birth."

2. Christian *discipleship* is the life of obedient following and faithful imitation of Jesus Christ. Fundamentally, discipleship has three tasks or dimensions. First and foremost is the cultivation of a life in the presence of God—both as an individual who prays, meditates and studies Scripture, and as a member of a community of disciples. Second, it is the ongoing proclamation of the gospel of Jesus Christ to others and, more broadly, a continual effort to give all of our speech and communication the character displayed in the Word of God. Third, discipleship is the ongoing participation in specific efforts to heal the afflicted of the earth and battle the demonic forces of our age. More broadly, it is an active determination to bring all of our activities, including our work and politics, into line with the loving, redemptive acts of God.

3. Christian growth implies a life characterized by taking *risks in faith*, raising and answering *questions* in the presence of God. Without the willingness to attempt "the impossible" at the call of God, the authentic Christian life cannot be experienced, for it is, in itself, impossible for the natural man or woman. So, too, growth in discipleship means bringing all of our questions to God, not least in regard to the will of God for our daily life and work. Equally important is the reverse process of allowing God to question us, to raise his agenda and priorities with us, as uncomfortable as that might be.

4. The Christian *church* is fundamentally an identifiable assembly of disciples founded on Jesus Christ and wholly centered on the worship of the One who died and rose again for our redemption. Jesus is the "cornerstone" of a foundation of the prophets and apostles, mediated today by Holy Scripture. Building up from this foundation and radiating out from the table of the Lord at the center, the church is also a learning, caring, witnessing, discipling and freeing community of brothers and sisters.

5. Christian disciples experience the intimate presence of Jesus Christ both in *mountaintop experiences* of the glory of the Lord and in the humble daily tasks of *servanthood*, "washing each other's feet." It is essential for disciples to withdraw from ordinary distractions to "seek the face of the Lord," though mountaintop experiences are exceptional in our discipleship. The ordinary, ongoing experience of walking close to Jesus Christ is found in humble servanthood; joyful, voluntary, willing even to endure hardship or suffering.

6. *Failure and defeat*, in the attempt to live as faithful disciples, are a sad fact of existence in a world still out of joint with God. Lack of preparation, overconfidence, failure to watch and pray, reliance on the weapons of the world, distance from Christ, nearness to the enemy, and self-concern are often the steps toward vulnerability and failure. At its worst, failure consists of denying that Jesus Christ is our Lord.

7. Despite our most serious betrayals and failures, God is prepared to forgive and restore us, to help us get up off the ground in a rousing comeback. The path to *recovery* includes an honest recognition of our failure and poverty of spirit. Recovery requires true repentance and mourning, meekness and quiet, a renewed hunger and thirst for the presence of God, a determination to remain in the community of faith, a decisive confrontation with Christ about the failure, and a testing of our recovery by beginning again the works of discipleship we were called to before our defeat. Self-pity and a flight from the Lord and the church can never lead to recovery.

8. *Evangelism*, the archetypical form of proclaiming the kingdom of God, is closely associated with actions and events that give substance and integrity to the message. The message itself is always focused on

the person of Jesus Christ. *Apologetics* has no independent significance; it only has value as a loving provision of reasons for the truth about Jesus Christ. Transformed behavior, historical eyewitness testimony, and the witness of the world view of biblical prophecy are the three primary avenues of apologetics. Faithful evangelism (and apologetics) may result in opposition or modest "first encounters." The disciple hopes that evangelism results in the growth of a church which is alive in prayer, sharing, worship, hospitality, learning the apostles' doctrine and witnessing.

9. The ongoing battle for *healing* the afflicted of the world is a veritable battle against demonic *principalities and powers*. In particular, the temptation to turn money into an idol, Mammon, the tendency of the political order to become demonic Babylon, and the crushing threat of disease, affliction and death must be battled and resisted in the name of Jesus Christ and in the power of the Holy Spirit. Christian disciples are called to be aware of this battle and participate in the forces of the Lord wherever they may work or live.

10. Christian disciples are gathered into a church that must strive for the difficult combination of generous, liberating *ecumenicity* with *discipline* and the true care and cure of souls. Outsiders must be sought and added to the church. Old guards must be softened by the work of Christ. Vital, caring, pastoral leadership must be nurtured and recognized in order to get beyond the impasse of a loose ecumenicity or a legalistic exclusivism.

11. Throughout the Christian life, especially in the face of opposition and *suffering*, disciples need instruction in the great and glorious dimensions of God's work in Jesus Christ, and the commensurate responsibility placed on his followers. Growth is essential. The obedient, imitating disciple seeks to manifest faith, hope and love. He or she grows in understanding of the church and of the meaning of servanthood in relationships. Disciples must be prepared to do God's good even when the cost is suffering. They must be infused with hope through the faithful care of authentic shepherds of Christ's flock.

12. Finally, Christian disciples must be prepared to recognize and resist *false teaching* and treasonous behavior in their midst, even if it comes from among their teachers and leaders. Growth in the Chris-

tian moral life and in knowledge of Jesus Christ is the primary preparation for disciples to weather such storms. The whole of the Christian life is to be lived out in an atmosphere of hope, anchored in both
the resurrection of Jesus Christ and the sure promise of his return.

These twelve points, even in their fuller development in previous
chapters, are not the whole story of biblical revelation or the Christian
life. Peter was not the only rock in the foundation of the church,
whose cornerstone is Jesus Christ. But, in the end, he turned out to
be a solid rock and not a "stumbling stone" or "rock of offense." May
God make each of us into a rock like Peter. The God of Jacob and
Simon is still among us. It is because this God we know in Jesus Christ
is *the* Rock that we have the continuing possibility of personal transformation in the faith, hope and love of Christian discipleship.

> I love you, O LORD, my strength.
> The LORD is my rock, my fortress and my deliverer;
>   my God is my rock, in whom I take refuge.
>   He is my shield and the horn of my salvation, my stronghold.
> I call to the LORD, who is worthy of praise,
> and I am saved from my enemies.
>
> As for God, his way is perfect; the word of the LORD is flawless.
> He is a shield for all who take refuge in him.
> For who is God besides the LORD?
>   And who is the Rock except our God?
> It is God who arms me with strength and makes my way perfect.
> He makes my feet like the feet of a deer;
>   he enables me to stand on the heights.
>
> The LORD lives! Praise be to my Rock! (Ps 18:1-3, 30-33, 46)

For Reflection or Discussion

1. Under what circumstances today do people suffer for Christ? Is there such
a thing as a Christian life without pain or suffering? Explain.
2. In what ways is the church today (your church, for example) most vulnerable to false teaching? What can you do about it?

3. How does the promise of the return to Jesus Christ affect the way you live and think?

4. As you studied about Peter in the previous chapters, what did you find most challenging or helpful? What are you going to do about it?

Notes

Chapter 1: The Promise of Peter: An Introduction

[1]What follows is a brief, synoptic overview of Peter's life as background for the more detailed studies which come in the following chapters. While this sketch is controlled by the New Testament evidence, it obviously includes a number of interpretative judgments on my part, not all of which I can take the space to defend.

[2]G. Dalman, *Sacred Sites and Ways* cited in Oscar Cullmann, *Peter: Disciple, Apostle, Martyr*, trans. Floyd V. Filson (Philadelphia: Westminster, 1953), p. 22, n. 28.

[3]F. J. Foakes-Jackson, *Peter, Prince of the Apostles* cited in Cullmann, *Peter*, p. 22, n. 29.

[4]For the broader historical background to the story of Peter, see F. F. Bruce, *New Testament History* (New York: Doubleday, 1969).

[5]I am, of course, assuming that the unnamed "disciple whom Jesus loved" in John's Gospel, John the son of Zebedee, and the author of the Gospel and letters of John are all the same person. This position has both advocates and critics.

[6]For scholarly evidence and arguments regarding Peter's possible relations to Rome, Mark's Gospel and 1 Peter, see Oscar Cullman, *Peter*; Raymond E. Brown, Karl P. Donfried and John Reumann, eds., *Peter in the New Testament: A Collaborative Assessment by Protestant and Roman Catholic Scholars* (New York: Paulist, 1973); D. W. O'Conner, *Peter in Rome: The Literary, Liturgical and*

Archaeological Evidence (New York: Columbia University, 1969); and the many commentaries and introductions to the New Testament material. A more popularly written work which argues the same position I have with regard to Mark and 1 Peter is J. B. Phillips, *Peter's Portrait of Jesus: A Commentary on the Gospel of Mark and the Letters of Peter* (New York: Collins and World, 1976).

[7] Against the majority opinion of New Testament scholars, I am closely in agreement with E. Michael B. Green, *Second Peter Reconsidered* (London: Tyndale, 1961); and idem, *The Second Epistle of Peter and the Epistle of Jude* (Grand Rapids, Mich.: Eerdmans, 1968).

[8] Cullmann, *Peter*, devotes eighty-two pages to a painstaking review of all the evidence, biblical and extrabiblical, for Peter's martyrdom in Rome. See also O'Conner, *Peter in Rome*.

[9] Note well, I am not saying that we should not study Paul! To the contrary, he deserves all the attention and respect we can give him. I am merely pointing out an imbalance in the amount of attention directed toward Peter and Paul (in favor of the latter); I am also suggesting that many Christians may be able to identify better with Peter than Paul.

[10] James D. G. Dunn, *Unity and Diversity in the New Testament: An Inquiry into the Character of Earliest Christianity* (Philadelphia: Westminster, 1977), p. 385.

[11] Cullmann, *Peter*, pp. 68-69.

[12] F. F. Bruce, *Peter, Stephen, James, and John: Studies in Early Non-Pauline Christianity* (Grand Rapids, Mich.: Eerdmans, 1979), pp. 42-43.

[13] For example, see W. T. P. Wolston, *Simon Peter: His Life and Letters* (Edinburgh: 1892); Clarence E. Macartney, *Peter and His Lord* (Nashville: Cokesbury, 1937); F. B. Meyer, *Peter: Fisherman, Disciple, Apostle* (London: Marshall, Morgan and Scott, 1939); and E. Schuyler English, *The Life and Letters of St. Peter* (New York: Our Hope, 1941).

[14] See the works by Cullmann, O'Conner, and Brown, *et al*, cited above, n. 6, and F. F. Bruce, n. 12 above. Another important scholarly study is H. N. Ridderbos, *The Speeches of Peter in the Acts of the Apostles* (London: Tyndale, 1962).

Chapter 2: Beginnings: The Meaning of Conversion

[1] Dietrich Bonhoeffer, *The Cost of Discipleship* (New York: Macmillan, 1963).

[2] Cullmann, *Peter*, p. 66. Cullmann makes the fascinating observation with respect to the doctrine of Jesus' atonement for human sin: "I am inclined to ascribe to Peter this particular and fundamental insight." He bases this judgment on Peter's first letter and his sermons in Acts.

Chapter 3: Three Tasks: The Content of Discipleship

[1] Richard J. Foster, *Celebration of Discipline: The Path to Spiritual Growth* (San Francisco: Harper & Row, 1978) is, deservedly, a modern classic on the

various inward, outward and corporate spiritual disciplines—a great study with good suggestions of where to turn for further help. See also Richard Lovelace, *Dynamics of Spiritual Life* (Downers Grove, Ill.: InterVarsity Press, 1979).

²John Bright, *The Kingdom of God* (Nashville: Abingdon, 1953) is still an excellent introduction to the Old Testament background to the preaching of the kingdom.

³George Ladd, *The Presence of the Future*, 2nd ed. (Grand Rapids, Mich.: Eerdmans, 1964) remains one of the best introductions to New Testament eschatology, especially Jesus' proclamation of the kingdom.

⁴John Howard Yoder, *The Politics of Jesus* (Grand Rapids, Mich.: Eerdmans, 1972) provides a masterful discussion of the "this-worldly" and social dimensions of Jesus' way. He connects his discussion of the Gospels with various texts in Paul's writings, in very helpful ways.

⁵I am not suggesting that Peter and his colleagues necessarily felt that their commission to proclaim the gospel of the kingdom implied a critique of how someone hawked fish in the Bethsaida market! I am arguing (a) that this was and remains one of the three great tasks of Christian discipleship, and that concretely and simply this always means talking to people about Jesus Christ; and (b) *from our perspective*, with the whole biblical teaching available, it is important to see this simple commission as the heart of a much broader, all-encompassing perspective in which God's Word is the standard and norm by which human words are to be judged—in relation both to their content and form.

⁶"The New Testament consistently views Jesus as a healer. Indeed, this healing mission is viewed as *one dimension of a larger confrontation with the effects* of sin on human life. . . . Jesus not only heals physical ailments, but he casts out demons, tames the angry sea, combats hunger and economic injustice, and even raises the dead." Richard J. Mouw, "Biblical Revelation and Medical Decisions," *Journal of Medicine and Philosophy* 4, no. 4 (1979), pp. 367-82. Reprinted in Stanley Hauerwas and Alasdair MacIntyre, eds., *Revisions: Changing Perspectives in Moral Philosophy* (Univ. of Notre Dame, 1983), pp. 182-202. The quotation is from p. 193 (my emphasis added).

I will have more to say about the demonic powers and healing in chapter ten below. As for the specific forms of the healings in the New Testament, I accept the truth of the details given in the text. Perhaps Jesus, Peter and their colleagues worked this way because its vividness (commanding crippled people to get up and walk, multiplying loaves and fishes and so on) was needed to get the attention of that generation. What I do *not* accept is the notion that only healings which copy these vivid details from the New Testament deserve to be called supernatural, divine or Christian healing. I believe that all life and all healing is from the hand of God and equally supernatural in origin. We are all different, I suppose, but I for one am not one bit more impressed by someone being healed at the command and prayer of another (I know people who have been healed like this) than I am with a highly trained doctor and nurse sacrificing career and financial opportunities in America in order to engage in health care in the Third World. Both, as far as I am concerned, are supernatural, unusual works of God's Spirit. And, note well, both can be imitated by evil spirits, human techniques and so on.

It is no more essential to limit the task of healing to spitting on the ground and commanding people to be well—than it is to limit "proclaiming the gospel" to speaking only Aramaic or Greek, wearing a toga, and broadcasting from Israel.

[7]I am not a member of the Charismatic movement nor am I a Pentecostal. But I cannot believe that God now has his hands tied and cannot give whatever sort of gifts and abilities to his servants that he wishes! God can do whatever he wants—and we do well to remain open to all possibilities rather than succumb to the narrow-minded naturalism of many people, especially intellectuals, in our century. Having said this, I am rather suspicious of purportedly Christian healers who (a) allow themselves to be promoted as "stars," (b) manipulate audiences emotionally with lights, music and so on, and (c) preach that everyone can and should be healed (and in the same fashion).

Chapter 4: Risks & Questions: Discipleship in Motion

[1]My debt to the thought of Jacques Ellul is perhaps greatest in this chapter. Ellul has a brilliant discussion of "risk and contradiction" in *The Ethics of Freedom* (Grand Rapids, Mich.: Eerdmans, 1976), pp. 355ff. His forthcoming book, *The Subversion of Christianity* (Grand Rapids, Mich.: Eerdmans, n.d.), contains a fine exposition of the modern thirst for security and fear of freedom; the idea that we must allow God to set the agenda and invite him to put us in question recurs in Ellul's work over the past forty years.

[2]We have three accounts of Jesus' walk on the water, each given immediately after the account of the feeding of the five thousand. Only Matthew adds Peter's walk on the water. All the accounts tell about Jesus coming to the disciples—only Mark adds that he "intended to pass them by." I regard Mark's phrase not as a conflict with the other accounts but as an additional detail helping us understand what the composite portrait might contain.

[3]One of the finest studies of Jesus' teaching and example with respect to prayer is the old devotional classic by Andrew Murray, *With Christ in the School of Prayer* (Westwood, N.J.: Revell, 1953).

[4]This event does not need to be reduced so that its *only* meaning is as a historical anecdote proving Jesus' deity. Rather, it is *also* a paradigm of the

movement of faith in relation to Jesus and the natural world around us. By no means is this a wild concept of faith having only this story as biblical backing! But, I contend, this is a great story for getting a handle on the risk of faith.

[5]My sections on Peter's questions and answers are summaries of the many "incidental" references to him in the Gospels. In addition to the major events studied in this book, there are many other references to Peter. Most of these are instances of his raising questions or being questioned by Jesus. A study of what followed from these questions is what justifies my including "the question" as an essential manifestation of the "risk of faith" and the style and tone of ordinary discipleship.

Chapter 5: Building on the Rock: The Meaning of the Church

[1]Ralph Martin, *The Family and the Fellowship* (Grand Rapids, Mich.: Eerdmans, 1979). Martin, a New Testament scholar, has given us some of the very best studies of the meaning and activity of the church. For additional perspective on church renewal and reform, it is hard to beat Howard Snyder's works, especially *The Problem of Wineskins* (Downers Grove, Ill.: InterVarsity Press, 1975) and *The Community of the King* (Downers Grove, Ill.: InterVarsity Press, 1977).

[2]Oscar Cullmann concludes that the saying ought to be accepted as genuine with Jesus (that is, not invented later and attributed to him by Matthew), but (unnecessarily, I think) he believes that the occasion of the Last Supper in the upper room is a more plausible setting than Caesarea Philippi.

The Greek word translated "church" *(ecclesia)* was an ordinary vocabulary word for an assembly of people—for political deliberation or other purposes. Although the biblical imagery is often one of a building or temple, it is essential to think of the church as an assembly of human beings. These people *are* a kind of building; the buildings in which they meet are not the church.

[3]On this subject see John Howard Yoder, "Binding and Loosing," *Concern* pamphlet no. 14 (Elkhart, Ind.: Goshen Biblical Seminary, 1967); also Cullmann, *Peter*, pp. 204-5.

[4]I will have more to say on "binding and loosing" in chapter eleven, and a case study in recovery from failure in chapter eight.

[5]Cullmann has argued this in his book *Early Christian Worship* (London: SCM, 1953), see especially pp. 29ff.

Chapter 6: Mountaintop & City Street: The Two Experiences

[1]Aldous Huxley, *Brave New World* (London: Panther Books, 1977), p. 73.

[2]The primary purpose of the transfiguration was undoubtedly to bear divine witness to the glory and deity of Jesus Christ as beloved Son of God the

Father. Nevertheless, I maintain that in most of Scripture there is more than one level of meaning and interpretation. If Peter is viewed as a kind of model of discipleship, we can look at this story from his vantage point: a disciple seeks after the presence of his Lord and observes him in his glory. I am not especially mystical by nature, and I do not think that the pursuit of extraordinary mystical "highs" is wise. However, I do think that the pursuit of God and his presence is important—through prayer, hearing God speak to us through the Word, and reflection.

[3]The transfiguration experience was an exceptional revelation of the glory of the Lord in very vivid form. What I wish to stress, by turning in the same chapter to the foot-washing episode, is that the Lord is *equally* present with us in our humble daily servanthood, though the experience lacks the sensational dimension of the mountaintop. Foot washing is, I would argue, an important example of servanthood for followers of Jesus.

[4]I offer this suggestion because it does seem odd that no mention is made of "masters" in this context. Certainly some Christians in the early churches were masters (for example, Philemon). Possibly the particular churches 1 Peter is addressed to were composed of slaves and poor people (though the reference to expensive adornments worn by women flies against this; compare 3:3). It remains an open question.

Chapter 7: Autopsy of a Defeat: The Great Denial

[1]For what follows we have much more information from all four Gospels than for any other part of this study. That alone is good reason to pay close attention to what happened. It is usually—but not always—easy enough to see how the composite account fits together. What follows is my best attempt to present an accurate reconstruction of the events.

Chapter 8: Prescription for a Recovery: Peter's Stunning Comeback

[1]The text says that the man on the shore was unrecognized (it turned out to be Jesus, of course). My suggestion that it was Zebedee is only in the interest of trying to understand why veteran fishermen, presumably tired after an unsuccessful night of fishing, would follow so quickly the labor-costly idea of an unrecognized stranger on the shore!

[2]As I say, a distinction between *agape* and *phileo* along the lines of the traditional interpretation is not *certainly* justified, because (a) John does not consistently employ them in a way that guarantees such a distinction in intended meaning, and (b) Jesus was presumably speaking Aramaic anyway, and (as I understand it) such a distinction does not have the same force in that vocabulary. Still, there *is* a difference between these Greek words for love, and I have difficulty believing that John *arbitrarily* changed them during the paragraph. The context invites us to think the change was intended

and meaningful. Maybe Jesus' tone of voice and emphasis was communicating something that John represented by the change of Greek words. (One sample text where there is a clear differentiation and development between these terms is 2 Peter 1:5-7, "Add to . . . your brotherly kindness *[phileo]*, love *[agape].*") It is, however, the *context* that suggests differentiating these terms for love in John 21—just as it is the context that suggests blurring the distinction between *petros* (rock) and *lithos* (stone) in my earlier discussion of the church. I offer this as a suggestion, however, and not as the argument of New Testament scholarly expertise.

³Traditionally, Peter is pronounced "restored" after this second stage (the encounter with Jesus). Certainly this is the pivotal episode, but I think that in light of the biblical stress on displaying our faith in our works (and in light of the text I will discuss from Rev 2), we only complete the picture of Peter's comeback by looking at what I call stage three.

Chapter 9: Charismatic Witness: Evangelism and Apologetics

¹On evangelistic methods in the New Testament, see the excellent studies by E. Michael B. Green, *Evangelism in the Early Church* (Grand Rapids, Mich.: Eerdmans, 1970); and Robert C. Coleman, *The Master Plan of Evangelism* (Old Tappan, N.J.: Revell, 1963). Also very helpful is Rebecca Manley Pippert, *Out of the Saltshaker* (Downers Grove, Ill.: InterVarsity Press, 1979).

²See Jacques Ellul *The Technological Society* (New York: Alfred Knopf, 1964); *The Presence of the Kingdom* (New York: Seabury, 1967); Ellul's recent study, *The Humiliation of the Word* (Grand Rapids, Mich.: Eerdmans, 1985), provides the background for an interesting discussion of the proclamation of the gospel in a society glutted by visual images.

³F. F. Bruce, *The Defense of the Gospel in the New Testament* (Grand Rapids, Mich.: Eerdmans, 1959), is a good place to begin further exploration of apologetics. Some interesting samples of modern apologetics: C. S. Lewis, *Mere Christianity* (New York: Macmillan, 1960) and *Miracles: A Preliminary Study* (New York: Macmillan, 1947); Francis A. Schaeffer, *The God Who Is There* (Downers Grove, Ill.: InterVarsity Press, 1968) and *The Church at the End of the 20th Century* (Downers Grove, Ill.: InterVarsity Press, 1970). In my opinion, the former was Schaeffer's most stimulating book; the latter was his best and most convincing. See also John Warwick Montgomery, *History and Christianity* (Downers Grove, Ill.: InterVarsity Press, 1965); and Clark H. Pinnock, *Reason Enough* (Downers Grove, Ill.: InterVarsity Press, 1980).

⁴My colleague William A. Dyrness has been eager to correct this myopia; see *Christian Apologetics in a World Community* (Downers Grove, Ill.: InterVarsity Press, 1983).

⁵I think this was said with at least a touch of humor!

⁶See Francis A. Schaeffer, *The Mark of the Christian* (Downers Grove, Ill.:

InterVarsity Press, 1970); also contained in Schaeffer's *The Church at the End of the 20th Century*. Most Christian converts that I know (or know about), including intellectuals, were won to Christ not by powerful arguments but by hearing about Jesus Christ from someone or some community that demonstrated extraordinary interest, care and love.

⁷The historical-evidence apologetic is given, for example, in J.N.D. Anderson, *Christianity: The Witness of History* (London: Tyndale, 1969); F. F. Bruce, *The New Testament Documents: Are They Reliable?* 5th ed. (Grand Rapids, Mich.: Eerdmans, 1960); and John Warwick Montgomery, *History and Christianity*.

⁸There are many studies available on the fulfillment of the ancient prophecies in Jesus. On the broader matter of developing a Christian world view, see Arthur Holmes, *Contours of a World View* (Grand Rapids, Mich.: Eerdmans, 1983); James Sire, *The Universe Next Door: A Basic World View Catalog* (Downers Grove, Ill.: InterVarsity Press, 1976). The great contribution of Francis A. Schaeffer was to call so persuasively for development of a broad and deep biblically informed Christian world view. Even if he was not wholly successful in fulfilling his ambitious program, he deserves our praise for almost singlehandedly provoking thousands of Christians to think more biblically, broadly and creatively.

Chapter 10: Battling the Powers: Sharing, Liberating and Healing

¹On the general subject of the principalities and powers, see Hendrik Berkhof, *Christ and the Powers* (Scottdale, Pa.: Herald Press, 1962); John Howard Yoder, *The Politics of Jesus* (Grand Rapids, Mich.: Eerdmans, 1972); Jacques Ellul, *The New Demons* (New York: Seabury, 1975); *The Ethics of Freedom* (Grand Rapids, Mich.: Eerdmans, 1976); and *Apocalypse: The Book of Revelation* (New York: Seabury, 1977).

²Jacques Ellul, *Money and Power* (Downers Grove, Ill.: InterVarsity Press, 1984) is a fascinating study of money and wealth in Scripture. See also Ronald J. Sider, *Rich Christians in an Age of Hunger* (Downers Grove, Ill.: InterVarsity Press, 1977); and John White, *The Golden Cow* (Downers Grove, Ill.: InterVarsity Press, 1979).

³On politics and the state, see Oscar Cullmann, *The State in the New Testament* (New York: Scribner, 1956); Yoder, *The Politics of Jesus*; Richard Mouw, *Politics and the Biblical Drama* (Grand Rapids, Mich.: Eerdmans, 1972); Jacques Ellul, *The Political Illusion* (New York: Random House, 1972); and idem, *The Politics of God and the Politics of Man* (Grand Rapids, Mich.: Eerdmans, 1972).

⁴What I am saying is that whether you are a senator, a member of the urban housing commission, a voter, an anarchist, or *whatever* your political place, these four perspectives remain the command of God.

⁵There is much literature on the problems of evil, suffering, pain, healing, and the goodness and power of God. Two studies that I have found helpful

are John Wenham, *The Goodness of God* (Downers Grove, Ill.: InterVarsity Press, 1974); and C. S. Lewis, *The Problem of Pain* (New York: Macmillan, 1982).

[6]In my view the important factors are to be under the command and in the power of Jesus the Lord and to do whatever we can to bring healing and care to the afflicted. This is why even legislative action, nutritional counseling and agricultural programs might fill the bill. As for modern "faith healers" (like the late Kathryn Kuhlmann), I find a lot of the claims, methods and theology unbiblical and misguided. Nor am I any more impressed by a quick cure than a slower one. All real healing is divine, as I see it. Nonetheless, I believe God can intervene in the world however he sees fit, and it is incontestable that *some* people have been healed of their illness or injury in ways that closely resemble the first-century experiences.

Chapter 11: A Faithful Shepherd: Ecumenicity and Church Discipline

[1]The term *ecumenical* (meaning roughly "worldwide") in our era has been most often used in relation to large institutional efforts to unite denominations (for example, the World Council of Churches, National Council of Churches). The ecumenicity discussed in this chapter is on a grassroots level. This is because the New Testament account points us in that direction. Nevertheless, I suspect the same basic perspectives apply both to problems within a given church and problems between churches and denominations.

[2]An "old guard" is, of course, not necessarily composed of people of advanced years! It is often the case that misguided young zealots lead the forces of hard-nosed traditionalism and exclusivism.

[3]Ralph Nabour, *The Seven Last Words of the Church* (Nashville, Tenn.: Broadman, 1979).

Chapter 12: Hope & Truth: The Message of the Letters

[1]E. G. Selwyn, *The First Epistle of Peter* (London: Macmillan, 1946), p. 1. Selwyn has written five hundred pages of introduction and commentary on Peter's one hundred and five verses! A monumental achievement. Though knowledge of Greek is necessary to follow the commentary fully, it is worth time for study by any interested in 1 Peter.

Bo Reicke, *The Epistles of James, Peter, and Jude*, W. F. Albright and D. N. Freedman, eds., The Anchor Bible (Garden City, N.Y.: Doubleday, 1964), argues that 1 Peter might have been prepared as a baptism or confirmation "sermon," that is, as a summary of essentials to strengthen the faith of new Christians; Reicke has helpful historical background information in his commentary; Alan M. Stibbs, *The First Epistle General of Peter: A Commentary*, Tyndale New Testament Commentaries, ed. R. V. G. Tasker (Grand Rapids, Mich.: Eerdmans, 1959), is a fine, brief, inexpensive, evangelical commentary with fifty-five pages of introduction by Andrew Walls; J. N. D. Kelly, *A Commentary on the Epistles of Peter and Jude* (London: Black, 1969), sometimes concedes more to biblical critics than I would like, but on the whole Kelly's commentary is a gold mine of information, well written and positive.

²On 2 Peter, the commentaries by Reicke and Kelly (see preceding note) will provide two "mainstream" perspectives; for an evangelical and constructive viewpoint which I find much more persuasive, see E. Michael B. Green, *Second Peter Reconsidered* (London: Tyndale, 1961), and *The Second Epistle of Peter and the Epistle of Jude,* Tyndale New Testament Commentaries, ed. R. V. G. Tasker (Grand Rapids, Mich.: Eerdmans, 1968).

³Sharp readers will detect a possible contradiction! What I describe here is, I think, the *normal* case; my guess is that the false teaching denounced in 2 Peter may have arisen and become popular in a situation of growing persecution, partly as a means of evading that opposition. How so? Because the false teaching of 2 Peter allowed disciples to live in conformity to the world and reduced the gospel to a purely "spiritual" or "intellectual" affair (no threat to the Empire!). At any rate, I am not saying that false teaching and heresy flourish *only* in tolerant times.

⁴Of course confrontations (for example, Paul and Peter in Antioch), general hearings (for example, the Jerusalem Council) and direct denunciations (2 Peter 2) have their place. In terms of preparing the rank and file to faithfully resist false teaching, however, I think Peter's counsel is *always* important and *often* the best strategy to follow.

⁵Denying Christ was, of course, the focal point of Peter's own worst failure. See chapter seven.

⁶This and other themes and key texts in ethics which have been treated only in cursory fashion in this study will be developed much more fully in my *Evangelical Ethics: An Introduction* (in preparation).